All Decked Out...

REDWOOD DECKS

Ideas and Plans for Contemporary Outdoor Living

Tina Skinner

Schiffer Publishing Ltd

4880 Lower Valley Road, Atglen, PA 19310

Acknowledgments

This book owes its existence to the California Redwood Association, which opened its doors, and its files, to supply photos and reams of information. The staff there deserves credit for their relentless pursuit of beautiful decks everywhere, and their role in helping to create them.

Skinner, Tina.
    All decked out--redwood decks : ideas
and plans for contemporary outdoor living / Tina Skinner
        p.   cm.
    ISBN 0-7643-0510-7 (pbk.)
    1. Decks (Architecture, Domestic)--Design and construction - Amateurs' manuals. 2. Decks (Architecture, Domestic)--Designs and plans. 3. Redwood   I. Title.
TH4970.S546   1998
690'.893--dc21   97-48772
                                                      CIP

Book Design by Blair Loughrey
Typeset in Goudy Handtooled BT/Souvenir LT BT

ISBN: 0-7643-0510-7
Printed in China

Published by Schiffer Publishing Ltd.
4880 Lower Valley Road
Atglen, PA 19310
Phone: (610) 593-1777; Fax: (610) 593-2002
E-mail: Schifferbk@aol.com
Please write for a free catalog.
This book may be purchased from the publisher.
Please include $3.95 for shipping.

Try your bookstore first.

We are interested in hearing from authors with book ideas on related subjects.

Contents

Introduction

California living: These two words evoke images of perfect weather, outdoor barbecues, honed tans, and relaxed minds. In a sense, this book documents that lifestyle, presenting its architectural settings.

The deck has become part and parcel of the American dream, the outdoor extension of the home. Decks serve as entertainment centers for family and friends, as romantic retreats, as relaxation centers complete with hot tubs, and as quiet garden contemplation spots.

Further, as many of the projects featured in this book attest, decks are fairly simple do-it-yourself projects. Basic decks are a great way to learn simple construction skills. And yet, as other pictures in this book will prove, decks can also be as complex as the imaginations of the best architects.

The decks featured in this book come from all over the country—from New Orleans to New York, and from Minneapolis to the mountains of Colorado. Most, however, are concentrated on the West Coast, and all are made from California redwood.

Redwood is often used for decks because its beauty, durability, and dimensional stability make it a good choice for outdoor applications. Redwood and cedar are the only two widely available softwoods in the United States that are well suited for outdoor use, though other woods can be chemically treated for the same rot and insect resistant qualities.

All of the photos in this book were taken by the California Redwood Association, which works to promote the use of redwood produced by its member mills in California. These mills are all dedicated to responsible stewardship of their private redwood forests. However, the purpose of this book is not to promote the use of any particular type of wood. This book is meant to serve as a mother lode of ideas for anyone seeking to expand their homes, and their lives, into the outdoors.

For Beginners

Photos by Ernest Braun

With no previous carpentry experience, homeowner Jerome Loston transformed a weedy, worn-out backyard lawn in Hercules, California, into an inviting outdoor room for entertaining and family recreation. Using books and the advice of friends, he designed and built a redwood deck with two overhead shade shelters, a swing, and built-in benches and planters.

For Beginners 7

Fire and Water

Photos by Ernest Braun

Dennis and Tracie Compomizzo had entertaining in mind when they built this extension to their Redding, California, home. There are two focal points on their 600-square-foot deck, the most unusual being a "conversation pit" featuring a built-in, semi-circular bench section and a fire pit. The circular area also includes three built-in planters lined with galvanized steel. A section of the upper deck was extended and shaped into a curve to become a bar for seating and serving food and drinks. The other focal point, the spa, commands the upper deck level, and is adorned with an overhead trellis and a beautiful privacy screen with an intricate cutout by designer/builder Timothy R. Bitts. A second shade trellis over an existing concrete slab completes the setting.

Fire and Water

Grand Canyon Overlook

Photos by George Lyons

Derrick and Jeanne Procell had an area in their Milwaukee, Wisconsin, backyard which was shaded by mature trees and overlooked a canyon and a river below. They wanted to add a deck for al fresco conversation, dining, and enjoyment of the river's view and sounds. Designer Milt Charno worked around the existing trees in the canyon near Milwaukee, Wisconsin, projecting a deck among them that imparts a feeling of privacy. The deck is complemented by a curving flagstone path and colorful plants.

11

Amateur Might

Photos by Ernest Braun

When accomplished amateur furniture builder Henry Angeli decided to add a 420-square-foot redwood deck onto his Petaluma, California, home, he gave the details and craftsmanship a lot of attention. He and his wife, Tay, designed and built a series of four deck sections, two with built-in benches and trellises. The decks follow the natural grade, occupying three levels. The addition was designed to enhance pool-side and backyard outdoor living pleasure by providing areas that can be used for different activities and enjoyed at various times of the day. Finally, a fanciful redwood gazebo was placed across the pool from the deck.

Amateur Might

Bar Harbor

Photos by T.S. Gordon

Jerry Carpentieri, a professional building and remodeling contractor, designed and built his handsome wood house himself over a three-year period. Part of the project for this New City, New York, home was integrating the cedar siding with redwood landscaping. A redwood path wraps around the house, providing access to all entrances. Carpentieri also installed extensive redwood planters and retaining walls, along with special redwood outdoor lights. A focal point of his deck is an outdoor bar/barbecue center which incorporates cabinets for storage and a small refrigerator. Protection from the elements is provided by an overhead redwood canopy with recessed lighting.

Bar Harbor

Urban Sprawl
Photo by Maris/Semel

Half of a backyard in New Orleans, Louisiana, was given over to this sprawling, 320-square-foot deck built by Decks Unlimited, Inc. Features on this deck include a checkerboard floor pattern for added visual interest, two latticework redwood screens on either side for privacy, built-in planters, and an expansive staircase leading to the lawn.

Golf Digest
Photos by Dan Sellers

Decks Appeal was asked to create a redwood deck in a long, narrow backyard which is adjacent to a golf course. The family's homeowner association in Plano, Texas, insisted that the deck be esthetically pleasing and not visually obtrusive when viewed from the golf course. The family likes to gather, cook, dine, and entertain outside, but wanted a low-maintenance backyard with a minimum of lawn mowing and garden upkeep. The solution was several angular deck segments joined by curving walkways. The different modules are used as separate family and guest conversation and activity areas. To minimize gardening chores, un-decked sections were covered with white stones. Latticed redwood railings and benches accent the spa, and a latticed screen provides privacy from a neighboring house.

Steel Rails

Photos by Ernest Braun

This multi-level deck was built by Bob Kiefer as part of an overall landscape project for a large, Teaneck, New Jersey, yard. Rectangular posts form a pleasing contrast to rounded, brushed stainless steel rails. These rails, combined with the slender, 2 x 4, knot-textured redwood boards, lend a sleek, modern look to the deck. "Mini-walls" screen the deck from neighboring yards and tie it in with the siding on the house.

Home Entertainment Center

Photos by Kim Brun

This three-level, 1,150 square-foot deck was designed by L. Dennis Shields to serve as a total entertainment center and focal point for the backyard of a Laguna Hills, California, home. The first level, shaded by a custom-designed trellis, provides direct access to the house and space for outdoor dining. The second level features a spa and built-in butcher-block bench. A brick fire pit and built-in bench are special features on the lowest level. On ground level, a wet bar with ceramic tile counter provides space for bar ware and cooking utensils.

Home Entertainment Center

Home Entertainment Center

Let the Sunshine In
Photos by Peter Loppacher

Mr. and Mrs. Joe Merola of Huntington, New York, had a 1-1/3-acre wooded lot so dense with trees that it was impossible to grow grass. So they enlisted builder Edward Assa to design an 800-square-foot deck built off a greenhouse at the rear of the house to make their yard more useable. Special amenities of the project include a built-in bench and planter boxes integrated into the retaining walls. The owners have found themselves outside a lot since then—using the deck for outdoor dining and entertaining. A spa is next on their list of home improvements.

Let the Sunshine In

Full Integration

Photos by Ernest Braun

The owners of a new, upscale house in a Colorado subdivision asked Garth Hystad to design a warm and inviting addition to their home. They wanted to accommodate a hot tub, and since the backyard faced west, they asked for a pleasant place to sit to be shaded from the hot sun in the summer and from the wind and cold the rest of the year. Hystad came up with this handsome, three-tiered deck with a built-in spa and a solarium/sun room, which is partially enclosed in glass. Careful blending of the solarium addition to the house, imposing redwood and stucco columns, and stainless steel railings and accents color-coated to match the house trim helped to beautifully integrate this addition with the house.

Full Integration

Spas and Pools

Tub with a View
Photos by Marvin Sloben

This redwood deck addition was the final phase of extensive renovations on this Spanish ranch-style house in Escondido, California. The house is located on a hill and the owner, Dan Hightower, wanted a deck with a spa that would take advantage of a view down a valley toward San Diego without the obstruction of railings. He designed a flowing structure featuring cascading, wrap-around stairs. The long, wide steps provide easy access to the deck from the backyard and are used as seating for enjoyment of the view. The right section of the deck was enclosed with a railing to provide a private section off the master bedroom.

Tub with a View

Clever Construction

Photos by Colin McRae

Talented do-it-yourselfer Larry
Kuntz designed and built this
inviting, multi-level deck himself
in Pleasanton, California. The
structure is approximately 22 x 28
and consists of two levels, a shade
structure, a built-in bench, and
redwood spa surround. One of
Kuntz's goals in building the deck
was to have a nail-free surface, so
he used innovative Dec Klips
underneath wherever possible.
He used a diagonal chevron
pattern on the lower deck surface,
and contrasting 2 x 2 square
sections on the upper deck.
Lattice conceals the supporting
structure underneath.

That's Entertainment

Photos by Tom Rider

Mr. and Mrs. William Osborne had neighborhood parties and barbecues in mind when they asked builder John Hemingway to design this 23 x 23-foot deck with spa. The 8 x 9-foot acrylic spa is used daily by the Los Altos, California, owners and accommodates up to twelve people for parties. Electrical outlets for cooking, redwood post lights with remote control from the house, and an 8-foot privacy fence of 4 x 8-foot lattice panels are special features that make the deck ideal for entertaining. Special features of this compact entertainment center include a wet bar topped with ceramic tile, built-in benches with adjacent tables, and planter boxes lined with tin. Tile was also used as an accent for the benches and planter boxes and curved hot tub staves were incorporated into the bench backs for comfort. The deck and all amenities are of Clear All Heart redwood. A clear water repellent with mildewcide was applied to modify weathering. White decorative rock sets off the structure and countersunk aggregate rounds provide a path to the house.

In Place of a Pool

Photos by Ernest Braun

When high school teacher Warren Popp's children grew up and left home, he and his wife, Patricia, decided to remove an unused backyard swimming pool. This left a large hole in their concrete patio. In its place, Popp designed and built a sophisticated redwood deck, spa, and surrounding. Built-in benches on three sides of the deck accommodate guests and grandchildren. Intricate screens provide privacy and visual interest. A garden is created using built-in planters and overhead trellises, which shade the benches and support hanging plants. Popp, of Sacramento, California, rounded all the edges of his redwood structure and took great care with detailing and placement of hardware. He installed lighting that makes the deck as attractive by night as it is by day.

In Place of a Pool

In Place of a Pool

Final Slope
Photos by Tom Rider

When Mr. and Mrs. Sy
Lederman built their hillside
home in Mill Valley, California,
six years ago, they retained a
small space at the rear for a deck
and spa. The steeply-sloped site
was a major challenge, but
designer Eli Sutton achieved a
sense of spaciousness without
extensive excavation. The
resulting 330-square foot, two-
level deck is accessible directly
from the master bedroom suite
through sliding glass doors. It
features a 7-foot Grecian spa, a
built-in bench, planters which act
as a retaining wall, and a privacy
fence designed to allow filtration
of light and air. The far end of
the deck affords a spectacular
view of the surrounding hills.

Final Slope

Decking Out
Photos by Dan Sellers

The existing swimming pool at Mike and Debby Mullen's home in Dallas, Texas, was built partly out of the ground due to an elevation drop. They wanted to expand their outdoor living space by decking out into this sloped surround. Designer/builder Jamie Turrentine solved their problem by wrapping an approximately 800-square foot redwood deck three-quarters of the way around the pool. An existing tree was incorporated into the design, and brick paving was added to the remaining area. The redwood decking was applied diagonally for extra interest and a clean-looking, white metal railing was added for safety. A sheltered area was jogged out from the rest of the deck and raised a level to further define it. The sheltered deck's edges were softly curved, mirroring the latticed shade trellis above.

Skirting the Pool
Photos by Maris/Semel

A multi-level, redwood deck unites home and pool for Huntington, New York, homeowner Irene Shear. Designer Edward Assa included features like a built-in bench with a seat made from 2 x 4 lumber and movable planters. The deck is approximately 840 square feet and is situated around a kidney-shaped pool with a brick walk. The upper deck level uses diagonal decking for contrast and visual interest. The deck was built with Construction Common grade redwood, one of the economical garden grades of redwood. A burnt orange, semi-transparent stain was used to protect the deck and wood and to provide a uniform appearance.

Skirting the Pool 51

Into Shinto

Photos by Marvin Sloben

An existing concrete pool surround in La Mesa, California, was refined by covering one side of it with a curved, Japanese-style, approximately 10- by 45-foot redwood deck addition. The graceful design echoes a Japanese garden, and a waterfall and koi pond are located elsewhere on the property. The deck is accented by redwood railings featuring an interrupted motif along the top which is the Japanese symbol for clouds. A focal point of the design is the Shinto-style redwood entryway structure. In "Shinto" or typical design, all of the lines are straight, almost austere, as opposed to the Buddhist "Temple" style, which is more curved and embellished. The construction of the project is characterized by superb craftsmanship. The deck boards are fastened underneath for a no-nail surface, edges are routed or rounded off, and sophisticated mortise and tenon joints are used for the entryway structure.

Private Platform
Photos by Ernest Braun

This tranquil redwood deck addition in a rustic Northern California setting was built around an existing swimming pool. The goals of the design were to create an inviting, private setting that would blend with the wooded landscape. A tile walkway flanked by fieldstone walls leads to a redwood entry arbor and into the pool/deck area. The pool surround consists of three redwood deck sections. The middle deck is raised to create a bridge between the other two decks. The three levels overlap the pool slightly, creating a floating platform effect. Alternating 2 x 6 and 2 x 2 deck boards were used for extra design interest. Because the pool was located near a property line, privacy was a design consideration. The solution was a 7-foot-high redwood fence with louvered boards to allow views of the landscape while creating a screen.

Private Platform   55

Private Platform

Long Reflection

Photos by Ernest Braun

Doug and Lydia Pringle enjoyed their view of San Francisco Bay and a large lot covered with old oak trees, but part of their property was unusable because it was rocky and sloped 45 degrees. Landscape architect Scott E. Smith designed a gently curved, 13 x 50, 520-square foot redwood and brick deck, complete with black-bottomed lap pool and hot tub. An existing oak was incorporated into the design, adding shade and interesting pool reflections. An arbor with a curved top defines access to and from the house, and a semi-circular privacy trellis at the end of the pool screens the deck from the nearby street.

Long Reflection

Above Board

Photos by George Lyons

Dareld Riemer of Colgate, Wisconsin, wanted both a redwood deck and above-ground pool in the backyard of his Tudor-style home. To accommodate the steep slope, Milt Charno designed a series of angular levels to reach the new pool. The top level is 14 x 14 feet. It is connected to the house and is used for sunning and dining. A 3-foot wide, elevated deck/path leads from the sun deck to the lower deck levels. At the pool's edge, a built-in bench was incorporated.

Above Board

Cover-up Job
Photos by Ernest Braun

The upper level of this Redding, California, deck encases an above-ground pool, cleverly giving it the appearance of a custom, in-ground installation. Owner Jain Moon created this yard-filling deck, with the upper deck flowing into a lower conversation pit via three steps, which provide both transition and seating. A custom-made, octagonal redwood table is a design accent. To contain the pool, and for low-maintenance gardening, the deck was planned to cover the entire backyard. For privacy from neighbors and to bring plants into the environment, a fence/planter combination was placed around the edges and topped by shady redwood trellises. The entire deck installation, built of economical, knot-textured Construction Heart redwood, was stained gray to match the house siding.

62   Cover-up Job

Pavilions and Shade Shelters

Treading Water
Photos by Ernst Braun

Ron and Sharon Colgate wanted landscaping that would permit them to enjoy their superb country setting in Northern California's wooded, rolling hills near Yosemite National Park. Their first step was the installation of an 8 x 12-foot, swim-in-place Jacuzzi-jet pool. Designer/builder Bryan Hays then surrounded the pool with a suitable deck/shelter—a 3,000 square-foot deck with a raised platform for the watery centerpiece. The soaring redwood pavilion/shade shelter features arches and lattice accents, built-in benches and planters, and sturdy safety rails. The benches feature rounded backs and lattice inserts, echoing the design of the pavilion.

Treading Water

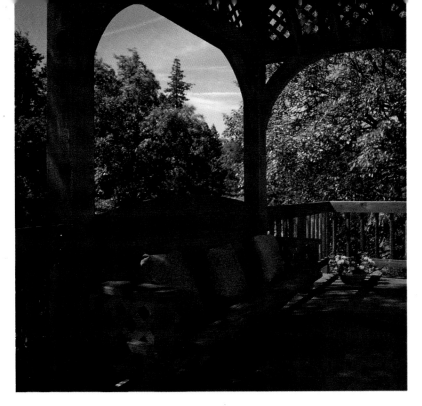

Trellis Retreat
Photos by George Lyons

Bonnie Brocker Beaudry designed this inviting pool-side retreat for Wayne and Carol Johnson of Menomonee Falls, Wisconsin. The angular deck features a built-in bench and shady overhead trellises, along with a fence enclosure that ingeniously disguises unsightly pool equipment. The surrounding cast-iron fence takes a humble backseat to the beautiful redwood construction.

Made in the Shade
Photos by Karl Riek

A shade pavilion is now the focal point in the two-acre backyard of Mr. and Mrs. Frank Wimer of Englewood, Colorado, who installed a 1,200 square-foot redwood deck with a pavilion and a spa. Located immediately off the kitchen, the deck functions as an outdoor room and a transition between the house and a brick-paved pool area. Features included by designer Sherry Dorward include bench seats, and a gate that complements the pavilion.

Defying Nature

Photos by Ernest Braun

Homeowners John and Susan Tomlinson wanted to create a backyard deck that would be cool and comfortable in the blistering Redding, California, summers and offer shelter in the wet winters. The solution was a 56-foot long, low-level deck nestled between a narrow concrete walkway and freeform rock gardens. One section of the deck contains an inviting spa. Three separate, pagoda-like pavilions create a dramatic focal point. Each has an asphalt-shingled hip roof supported by four concrete columns which were stuccoed to match the texture of the house.

High Tea

Photos by Ernest Braun

This unique teahouse/pavilion was created by custom craftsman and designer Robert Hauck. This project features a redwood deck connected to the adjacent San Martin, California, house by a boardwalk. Posts support a soaring overhead structure built with redwood and bluish-gray acrylic.

High Tea

Elegance Al Fresco
Photo by Ron Kolb

Designer Darin Moxley created a perched-in-the-woods ambiance with this 14 x 14 gazebo that soars 16 feet high in the center. Topping a 12-foot-high, raised redwood deck in Independence, Kentucky, the gazebo is supported by 6 x 6 posts. The arched sections are made of plywood, and the curved, Oriental-style roof is covered with asphalt shingles. A cooling ceiling fan and an antique weathervane complete the structure. The deck incorporates a built-in bench and a railing made more attractive by capital ball trim pieces and 2 x 2 spindles.

73

Outdoor Octagon
Photos by Jessie Walker

The owners of this house on a pleasant, spacious lot near Madison, Wisconsin, were devastated when a tornado wiped out twenty white oak trees aged between 100 and 200 years old. To replace the trees as a backyard focal point, they decided to create a romantic, redwood deck and gazebo. Builder Gregory Onsager worked with the owners to design this graceful, spacious structure. There are two octagonal pods—one adjacent to the household sun room, the second connecting the main deck to a set of stairs that leads to a nostalgic, 12-foot diameter octagonal gazebo. The angles and elevations fit the rolling terrain beautifully. The decking was sealed with a clear finish to showcase the natural color and textures of knotty garden-grade redwood, and the railings and trim were painted white for contrast.

Outdoor Octagon   75

Wind Breaker

Photos by Ernest Braun

Patrick and Michelle O'Brien's one-of-a-kind deck affords them a great view of the Rocky Mountains from their home on the outskirts of Denver, Colorado. The O'Briens wanted to create an addition that would handle large groups for cookouts, offer a good view, and still provide privacy and shade. Their solution was a 28-foot extension that connects to the main floor of their home, 8 feet above ground level. The deck is fully enclosed with railings and features a raised and offset entry platform to the house. The main deck has built-in benches for seating up to sixteen people. An unusual feature is the screened area at the south end of the deck. The wing-shaped roof is designed to withstand the high winds common in the Denver area during the spring and fall. For shade and privacy, the O'Briens added lattice panels between the roof supports. Shades of gray, white, and magenta stains were used to highlight design features and to blend with the color of the house. A unique stepping stone of poured concrete acts as landing to a stairway leading from the deck to the back yard.

Tree Pods
Photos by Ernest Braun

A steep, rocky backyard prevented these homeowners from enjoying their beautiful, wooded site in the San Francisco Bay area. Builder Bryan Brylka solved the problem with a modular decking system that allowed him to place three six-sided deck pods at different levels down the site. The units are connected by stairs and punctuated with alternating built-in benches and on-deck planters.

Tree Pods 81

Tree Pods

On Many Levels
Photos by Mark Becker

Shawn and Ken Demont had no usable outdoor living space. Their small front yard slopes straight into the street and the backyard was a patchwork of concrete, loose brick laid on sand, and weed-infested grass. Architect Mark Becker designed a 1,000-square foot, multi-level deck with built-in benches and planter boxes to provide attractive, functional, low-maintenance outdoor living space. Along the southwest wall, a free-standing stacked trellis was built to block afternoon sun and obstruct the view of houses on the hill above. Because the Demonts chose a natural, gray, weathered appearance for their deck, no finish was applied to the redwood.

Lights, Columns, Action
Photos by Marvin Sloben

Architect Craig Townsend was looking for an attractive way to expand his small house and to provide a natural transition into the backyard. He installed French doors, poured concrete ledgers, and hung a redwood deck addition off of these ledgers. The approximately 300-square-foot deck features interesting angles to add design interest and fit around existing plants and trees. Built-in bench/ platforms provide seating and areas to set up food and beverages for entertaining. Footings on one side of the deck were extended with concrete blocks, grouted, and plastered to create eight whimsical columns. The pillars are staggered to provide privacy from a neighboring house. Townsend made his own copper lights for the tops of some of the pillars.

Light Rail Traffic
Photos by Marvin Sloben

To disguise a badly deterio-
rated, 40-year-old concrete slab
outside this rustic mountain
home in Idyllwild, California,
designer/builder Scott Padgett
covered it with a graceful,
semicircular redwood deck.
The inviting, 550-square-foot
structure wraps around the
front and side of the home and
provides easy access to the
front door. To create a visual
break in the deck and to help
establish two distinct areas
without changing levels,
Padgett placed the 2 x 6 knot-
and sapwood-textured red-
wood boards in two directions.
Handmade outdoor lights and
lamps complete the setting.

Tree Incorporated

Photo by Ernest Braun

Dr. Robert F. Powers of Redding, California, had a huge blue oak in his side yard that he wanted to be the centerpiece of his new redwood deck. Because the slope was complex, the deck was laid out in a multi-level design. Powers, the designer and builder, created a series of broad, step-like tiers. This configuration lowered the main deck level around the tree and provided ample walking space under the branches.

87

Light Rail Traffic

Bent into Shape

Photos by Ernest Braun

Curves were one of Enrico Ricci's requirements when he set out to design and build his own deck in Salinas, California. One of his goals was to use the deck to decrease the angularity and white expanse of his house. He wanted to create a comfortable outdoor area so that his family could dine outside and enjoy open space and hill views. And he wanted it to be spacious enough for his children to play on and for entertaining. The curved fascia around the perimeter of the deck is formed with two layers of redwood benderboard glued together. A curved step platform from the kitchen door was also built with redwood benderboard, laid on edge and glued together.

Porched for Action

Photos by Leslie Wright Dow

This deck suits its Concord, North Carolina, setting, evoking Southern porch images while providing an open-deck atmosphere over-looking a golf course. John and Cindy Barnhardt's 600-square-foot curved deck was built over an existing concrete patio. Builder Alex Porter designed it with many porch-like elements, including a curved brick founda-tion, which is painted white to match the house, large, pilaster-like posts trimmed with decorative moldings on the top and bottom, shaped handrails, and painted balusters. The posts incorporate built-in lighting, and railing uprights alternate in size for extra interest. The top rail was left unpainted to integrate railing with floor surface.

Red on Redwood

Photos by Stephen Cridland

Steel piping with a powder-coated finish provides a striking, modern look for this home-improvement project in Portland, Oregon. Peter and Johanna Thoeresz wanted to replace an existing second-level deck on their 1950s Monterey-style house, and architect Garry Papers satisfied them with this. He replaced aluminum windows in the living room, dining room, and kitchen with French doors, giving access to the redwood deck from three major rooms. A hot tub was placed so that it is accessible from the kitchen, but out of sight from those eating or relaxing on the deck. Wooden frames were built to support wisteria vines, providing shade in the summer and letting light in during the winter months. He widened the existing deck with two pop-outs which accommodate seating and a table/eating area, in addition to adding design interest.

Red on Redwood 93

Tudor Details
Photos by Marvin Sloben

This beautifully-crafted deck addition to a Southern California house does a great job of looking as if it has always been there, echoing the Tudor architecture. Designer/builder Joseph D. Wood built the approximately 350-square-foot deck to create an inviting outdoor living space on a previously little-used side yard. The deck and a spa are neatly wrapped in redwood siding. Strikingly shaped railings feature a whimsical heart motif, and railing post capitals are hand carved. An overhead structure repeats the shape of the roof lines of the house and is a visual reminder of characteristic Tudor timbers. The structure was mortised and tenoned and pegged. All of the exposed redwood was stained with Olympic black oak stain to blend it with the Tudor trim of the house. This was top coated with a clear sealer.

94

95

On Different Levels

Photos by Ernest Braun

Gary and Lynn Cushenberry's home is situated in a beautiful, country setting in Belmont, California, on a lot covered with oak, bay, and laurel trees. They were not able to enjoy outdoor living, however, because of a severe slope. Mr. Cushenberry designed and built his approximately 1,000-square-foot redwood deck himself, wrapping it around three sides of his home and creating a variety of changing levels and stairs that echo the contours of his land. He was also able to design the deck to incorporate most of the existing trees. For extra design interest, he changed the direction of the boards at different levels and incorporated built-in benches and planters.

On Different Levels

Victorian Place
Photo by Peter Krogh

A series of new redwood decks and a screened porch added multi-level outdoor living space to this 1907 Victorian house in Chevy Chase, Maryland. The deck design was meant to echo the embellished trim on the house, to integrate it with the garden, and to provide more space for entertaining, dining, and family relaxation. The decks and porch overlook the modest garden, which was previously overshadowed by the 2-1/2 story rear facade of the residence. The first-floor deck was built in a semi-circular shape for extra design interest. The entrance from the house is from the family room through a redwood colonnade, which also supports the second-floor deck. A pair of curved stairs descend to the garden on either side of the porch, hugging the rounded forward bow. Latticework conceals the supporting structure under the deck and creates storage space. The shop-made picket railing and support posts with decorative ball caps were painted white to blend with house trim. The more angular, second-floor deck is accessed from the master bedroom.

99

Japanese Fire Pit
Photos by Ernest Braun

This large, curvilinear redwood deck wraps around two sides of a contemporary house in San Rafael, California. The 2,138-square-foot deck provides outdoor living and entertaining space for Douglas Rosestone's family of six, including a play area for children. Special features of the deck include a curved, laminated railing that extends around its perimeter, a built-in planter with overhead trellis, a 24-foot built-in bench, and a sunken, Japanese-style fire pit with an overhead structure of stacked timbers. A square grille of cross-lapped 3 x 3's suspended from overhead beams provides additional design interest and shade. Two built-in planter boxes are incorporated into the fire pit area.

Japanese Fire Pit   101

Japanese Fire Pit

Over the Autos
Photos by Barbeau Engh

Mr. and Mrs. Mervil Engh replaced an older deck with this 700-square-foot deck over their garage. Special amenities include built-in benches integrated with the railings and a specially designed planter box with movable, 2 x 2 slats that allow drainage and level changes. The planter box is faced with saw-textured redwood siding to match the house.

Low-down Deck

Photos by Marvin Sloben

When Richard and Karin Greenwood decided to add a deck to their redwood house in Idyllwild, California, they knew what they didn't want: they didn't want to block off the view they already had from their dining room table of a series of small waterfalls in the nearby, seasonal creek. So designer Scott Padgett created a home extension as low to the ground as possible, with a minimal railing height. He created two rectangular levels with a corner off of each to achieve a more interesting shape. He designed both freestanding and built-in benches with an eye toward comfort, and added unique "floating" stairs, which grow wider as they ascend.

Low-down Deck   107

Low-down Deck

Excavating for Hold

Photos by Marvin Sloben

Designer Gary McCook'had a lot of limitations when he set to work on a deck for Lee and Sharon Grissom of San Diego, California. Their back lot was steeply sloped, and their neighborhood homeowners' association restricted deck surfaces to a maximum 3-foot elevation. It was necessary, therefore, to excavate into the slope. A wide, 3-foot-high retaining wall was built, and designed to incorporate a seat. A planter wraps around an existing eucalyptus tree that was saved and incorporated into the deck structure. The stair and deck railings were painted white to echo the detailing of surrounding houses and give a contemporary look to the structure.

Following the Shoreline

Photos by Marvin Sloben

When designer/builder Scott Padgett took on a project for Arnold Leskin of Studio City, California, he set out to create a structure harmonious with the outdoor environment. The existing site, with more than 1,000 square feet of space to fill, is faced with a wooded area sloping away to a meandering stream. Padgett chose to let the waterway influence the deck's overall profile. The result is a floating, curved deck sculpture with five levels, incorporating rocks and trees on the site. The circular outer line of the redwood deck roughly corresponds to the creek's path below. The circular seating space cantilevers beyond the level area and over the creek for optimum enjoyment of the site. The deck is designed to facilitate large gatherings and yet contain smaller areas for intimate conversation. Mood lighting was accomplished by using low-voltage lights in 1/2-inch diameter clear plastic tubing, which was threaded through pre-drilled holds at the top of each 4 x 4 post before the cap rail was installed.

Cornered

Photos by Ernest Braun

This L-shaped bench transformed a bare corner of a deck in Modesto, California, into an inviting conversation area. The 9 x 9-foot redwood structure features a hip roof that creates a shady retreat. The ample bench is nearly 3-feet deep and offers plenty of room for sitting and lounging. Seat cushions covered with all-weather fabric add comfort and style. Classic lattice panels for the back of the bench echo an adjacent latticed deck railing. The bench was finished with a semi-transparent white stain to harmonize with the bleached gray deck.

Oriental Expression
Photos by Tom Rider

When Donald and Nancy Chew
of Oakland, California, visited
China several years ago, they
photographed a staircase with a
classic Oriental lattice railing. A
few years later, the Chews
asked designer Peter Hirano to
replicate that railing, modifying
it to suit their new deck.

Plus Patio and Patina

Photos by Ernest Braun

The owners of this Berkeley, California, home had an upstairs deck with a fantastic view of the San Francisco Bay, but the deck was suffering from dry rot and it offered no access to the backyard. They also wanted a backyard patio and deck to enhance their enjoyment of their garden and view. They requested that craftsman Timothy Jones design a screen to hide a garden tool area at one end of the patio and a private seating area high enough to see over fruit trees. The new deck features an inviting, built-in redwood bench and screen topped by a pergola, with copper inserts into the screen that were chemically aged to a turquoise patina. The deck descends via a series of graceful steps to a lower redwood deck and then to a slate patio edged with terra-cotta tiles. A redwood screen at the edge of the patio conceals garden tools and features delicate latticework and more copper inserts. Jones's meticulous attention to quality and detailing is shown in the rounded edges of the redwood lumber and sophisticated construction techniques.

Plus Patio and Patina   117

Plus Patio and Patina

Rounded Out

Photo by T. S. Gordon

An existing, unattractive concrete slab patio in the backyard of this ranch house in Denver, Colorado, was covered and expanded with a stunning deck addition designed by Greg Dowdy. The approximately 600-square-foot deck features a cascade of curved steps placed in an "S" design and built-in planters.

Safety Features

Photos by Ernest Braun

Peter Wilson and Maryanne Cobb wanted a deck that would provide a safe play area for their small children, space for a dining table, plenty of seating, and a view of their backyard. They had several doors, and good circulation was also a criterion. Additionally, they wanted the design to echo the style of their charming, 1930s Craftsman-style, wood-shingled house in Berkeley, California. Designer Richard Schwartz pleased them with a 12 x 16 foot addition with a U-V-shaped extending bay, which is meant to be a conversation nook as well as a "child trap." Multiple, built-in benches are wrapped around the deck to create a feeling of intimacy. Two massive built-in planters provide nearby color and texture, and an overhead trellis provides shade and contributes to the cozy, enclosed ambiance. The unusual railing incorporates wood shingles to echo the house exterior and copper pipes, which will weather to match the color of the house trim.

Safety Features

Accessorizing

Photos by Ernest Braun

Mark and Connie Ciorio wanted drama, as well as useful features, for their existing deck. They frequently entertain for business, so it was important to have space. And they wanted to visually break up the large expanse of light-colored stucco on their two-story house. MR DECK™ of San Martin, California, incorporated lots of deck accessories to make the Diorio's deck interesting. These include an overhead trellis with angled end details to break up the house expanse and add architectural character. A bar/food service counter was located outside the kitchen window to make it easy to pass out refreshments. It features a built-in brass sink and brass hardware. A built-in, truncated round table is incorporated into one of the trellis support posts. Two redwood benches with hinged tops open for storage and provide seating. The existing deck and the new amenities were coated with a custom finish to blend old and new together. The bar and table tops were coated with an additional wax finish for extra protection.

Rails for Tails

Photos by Ernest Braun

Custom deck designer Robert Hauck created an angular, zigzag shape for this 16 x 70-foot deck in Portola Valley, California. It includes an appealing combination of lean-out railings and built-in benches, with 100 feet of continuous seating overlooking Northern California's hills and valleys.

126

Backyard Boardwalk

Photos by Charles Callister Jr.

The much-admired Sea Ranch development on the rugged Northern California coast has long been a showcase for unusual and spectacular design. The owner of this contemporary redwood Sea Ranch house wanted a landscaping solution that had the feel and serenity of a Japanese garden. Designer Katherine Klawans Smith designed an elegant series of redwood decks connected by a simple redwood boardwalk which crosses over a garden consisting of a small, recirculating stream, rock accents, stone paving, and carefully selected plants. A spa is incorporated into the garden design, as is a one-of-a-kind redwood burlwood table designed and built by Dave Elder. Lighting was installed for outdoor entertaining in posts lining the walkway.

Backyard Boardwalk

Design and Build Your Own Deck

Building a beautiful, custom deck is easier than you think. The following pages contain some simple, ready to build projects, as well as tools for custom designing decks for your home.

There are six simple projects detailed by the California Redwood Association—a basic 8 x 10 foot deck, a deck around a hot tub, a simple ground-level deck over concrete, a shade shelter, a butcherblock bench, and a planter.

In addition, the following pages contain deck modules and related elements on a scale of ¼-inch = 1 foot. These can be photocopied, cut-out, and arranged to suit your personal needs and tasts. Matching detailed blueprints give construction details and all the information you need to build each module. These will help you develop a complete shopping list for materials. In addition, you'll find detailed drawings for stairs, railings, and benches. These were drawn from the California Redwood Association's Design-a-Deck™ kit.

The California Redwood Association has made it really easy to create a deck with a Design-a-Deck™ kit. The kit comes complete with a plastic-coated design grid and static cling forms of deck sections and other amenities such as stair forms, tables, chairs, hot tubs, and planters that you can arrange to suit your home and its terrain. The kit is available for $19.50 and includes two illustrated booklets, one to help you visualize deck designs, and a construction guide with step-by-step instructions for building, comprehensive blueprints, and the grid and templates mentioned above. Other literature is available from the California Redwood Association for $1 or less. For a list of literature on garden, architectural, finishes, education and conservation issues, and other general topics, call the California Redwood Association at 415-382-0662 or write to them at 405 Enfrente Drive, Suite 200, Novato, California 94949.

Redwood 8×10 Deck

This small deck can make a big difference at a garden doorway, next to a retaining wall or under your favorite tree. It's relatively easy to build and won't cost too much either.

1 **Placement** First decide the placement and height of the deck. You can build a free-standing deck or one that is attached to the side of your house.

NOTE: The deck described here is free-standing. To attach the deck to a house, anchor one of the skirtboards to the house framing with the simplest anchoring system permitted by local building codes.

If the deck is adjacent to a house, it should be about 1-inch below the interior floor or a comfortable step down, usually about 7 inches.

2 **Corners** Mark the deck corners with stakes and string. Check the squareness of the projections by measuring between stakes. Then measure diagonally between the corners. If the two diagonal measurements are equal, the corners of the deck are properly marked.

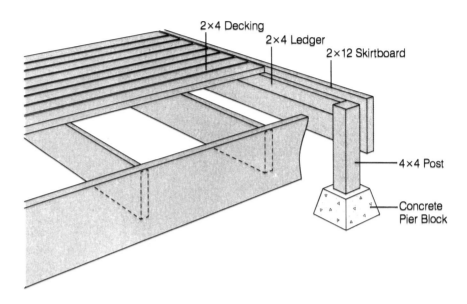

2×4 Decking
2×4 Ledger
2×12 Skirtboard
4×4 Post
Concrete Pier Block

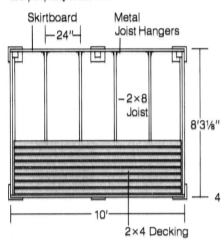

Skirtboard — 24"
Metal Joist Hangers
2×8 Joist
8'3⅛"
10'
2×4 Decking

3 **Posts** Place the posts in position. If you are using a ledger on the side of the house, you will need three posts. For a free-standing deck, you will need six. Post lengths will vary according to the contour of the ground. Establish the height at one

corner and use this to measure the others. Accurate measurement and trimming of the posts can be achieved using a string level or a carpenter's level. Post tops should be 2-inches below the top of the skirtboards. This provides room for the deckboards. Toenail posts to the nailing blocks of pre-cast concrete footings.

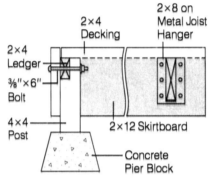

2×4 Decking
2×8 on Metal Joist Hanger
2×4 Ledger
⅜"×6" Bolt
4×4 Post
2×12 Skirtboard
Concrete Pier Block

4 **Skirtboards** Attach the 2×4 ledgers to the two 8-foot skirtboards with ⅜×2½-inch lag screws. The ledgers will support the ends of the decking. Bolt the skirtboards to the posts with ⅜×6-inch carriage bolts, washers and nuts.

5 **Joists** Attach 2×8 joists using metal joist hangers. Leave room so that the decking will be even with the top of the skirtboards. Space the joists 24 inches on center, which means the center of one joist is 24 inches from the next.

6 **Decking** Lay the 26 2×4 deckboards on the joists. Do not nail the boards in place until you are satisfied with their arrangement and spacing. Pre-drill nail holes near the ends of boards to prevent splitting. Nail decking in place.

Deck Materials

Description	Quantity	Size	Length
Construction Heart Redwood			
Posts	6 pieces	4×4	varied
Skirtboard	2 pieces	2×12	10 feet
Skirtboard	2 pieces	2×12	8 feet
Ledgers	2 pieces	2×4	8 feet
Joists	4 pieces	2×8	8 feet
Construction Common Redwood			
Deckboards	26 pieces	2×4	10 feet

Other Materials

Quantity	Description
1 lb.	16-penny nails
8	2×8 joist hangers
10	⅜×2½-inch lag screws
10	⅜×6-inch carriage bolts, washers & nuts
6	Concrete footings with nailing blocks

Use non-corrosive, hot-dipped galvanized, stainless steel or aluminum fasteners and hardware.

Redwood
Deck Over Concrete

Building a redwood deck over an existing concrete slab is an easy way to get the complete enjoyment of a deck at a fraction of the labor and cost. Concrete slabs that have been around for years are often cracked, uneven or just plain unsightly. Stable, weatherable redwood can cover all these defects beautifully.

There are two basic steps in Deck Over Concrete construction.

1 Attach Construction Heart redwood sleepers to the concrete slab.

2 Nail 2×4 or 2×6 Construction Common decking to the sleepers.

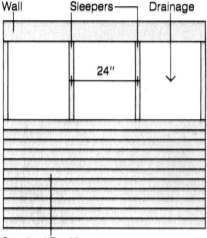

Standard Decking

1 **Sleepers** First lay the sleepers down roughly in the spots they will be attached. They should be spaced 24 inches on center. The sleepers may be random lengths because the concrete slab will support the full length of the sleeper. This can be a savings because short lengths are often less expensive. If the concrete slab is cracked or uneven this is the time to level the sleepers with shims or small pieces of Construction Heart redwood. If the concrete slab is adjacent to the wall of a house, sleepers should run perpendicular to the wall for best drainage.

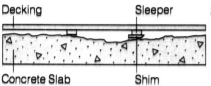

The best way to attach sleepers to the concrete slab is with a "power hammer" which uses explosive charges to shoot special nails into concrete. Power hammers are available at building supply and tool rental centers. They are easy to use and designed with safety features to help prevent accidents. Follow manufacturers directions for safe operation.

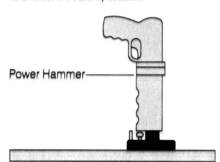

Power Hammer

2 **Decking** The decking should be laid in place before nailing. Random lengths of Construction Common can be used for decking as long as butt joints meet over the sleepers. It is good practice not to have two butt joints adjacent to each other on the same sleeper. Trim and nail boards individually, as opposed to trimming them all at once. This helps prevent mistakes and offers leeway to cover for miscalculations in measurement.

Nailing Use stainless steel, aluminum and top quality, hot-dipped galvanized nails and fasteners for exterior redwood projects. Cheaper corrosive or electroplated nails can react with redwood's natural chemicals to cause stains.

For 2-inch decking, use 10-penny nails. Decking nails should penetrate 1½ inches into the sleepers. Pre-drill holes at the ends of boards to avoid splitting. To allow for water drainage, decking boards should be spaced about ⅛ inch apart.

Materials Required For One Square (100 Square Feet)

Materials	Standard Decking
2×4 Construction Heart (sleepers)	60 Linear Feet
2×6 Construction Common (decking)	210 Linear Feet
2×4 Construction Common (decking)	326 Linear Feet

Redwood Deck Around Hot Tub

Redwood decks turn backyards into garden retreats and the addition of hot tubs makes them even better. Building a deck for a tub is very much like building any other deck. (See CRA booklet *Deck Construction.*) The most important thing to remember is that water is *extremely* heavy and the tub will need support independent of the deck.

The major elements for this deck around a tub are:

Footings Concrete pillars or pier blocks which support the weight of the entire deck.

Posts Vertical supports for the deck, attached to footings by drift pins or by toenailing. Construction Heart is recommended for its decay resistance. Bottoms of posts should be 6 inches off the ground.

Stringers straddle the posts and are attached with carriage bolts or lag screws.

Joists Horizontal supports nailed to stringers 2 feet on center, with 16d nails which support the decking. Blocking may be nailed between joists for stabilization.

Decking The surface of the deck; can be economical Construction Common grade lumber. Nail with one 16d nail per joist bearing in a staggered nailing pattern. Allow ⅛-inch space between deckboards for drainage.

Raised seating area can also serve as storage and can conceal plumbing. The basic element is the *wall unit* which rises 24″ above the deck. The decking should be ½″ below the tub rim. Build the five wall units first and then attach the other members following standard nailing methods in this order: ledgers, joists, blocking, facing and then decking.

The access hatch consists of 2×4's or 2×6's attached to a simple box frame. The frame should measure approximately 22¼×20¾ inches so that it fits securely into the stud wall. Although the hatch can be removable, a hinge is the easiest way to attach it to the stud wall unit.

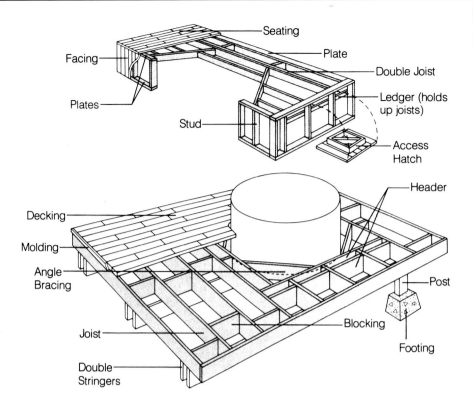

Deck Around Tub Materials

Construction Heart Redwood

Description	Quantity	Size	Length
Posts	9	4×4	height of deck
Stringers	4	2×10	16 feet
	2	2×10	7 feet
	2	2×10	2 feet
Joists	6	2×6	12 feet
	1	2×6	7 feet
	6	2×6	26 in.
Blocking	12	2×6	2 feet
Angle Braces	4	2×6	3 feet
Headers	2	2×6	8 feet
	2	2×6	16 feet

Construction Common Redwood

Description	Quantity	Size	Length
Decking		2×6	240 lin. ft.
Trim		1×2	56 lin. ft.

Framing Details 12′×16′ Deck

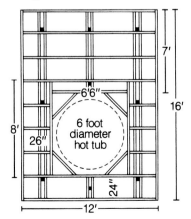

Raised Seating Area Materials

Construction Heart Redwood

Description	Quantity	Size	Length
Plates	2	2×4	12 feet
	4	2×4	8 feet
Studs	21	2×4	2 feet
Joists	2	2×6	12 feet
	5	2×6	4 feet
	2	2×6	3 feet
	2	2×6	2 feet
Ledgers	2	2×6	6 feet

Construction Common

Description	Quantity	Size	Length
Facing		1×6	124 lin. ft.
Decking		2×6	124 lin. ft.

Other Materials

Description	Quantity	Size
Nails (non-corrosive)	5 lbs.	16d common
	12 lbs.	16d box
Lag Screws and Washers	36	⅜×4 inch

Raised Seating Area

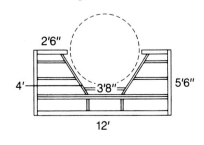

Redwood
Shade Shelter

This handsome redwood shelter will shade your deck or patio, making it cool and comfortable. In fact, it can help your whole house stay cooler by shielding windows, walls and sliding glass doors from the sun.

Building a shade shelter is relatively easy. Here are plans that can be modified for specific applications.

1 **Ledger** Anchor the 2×4 ledger to the house framing using lag screws. Screws should penetrate into studs or header to provide proper support. The ledger should be Construction Heart grade redwood. Make sure there is enough room between the ledger and eaves of the house for the 2×6 joists.

2 **Posts** Prepare footings for the posts. The type of footing for posts will vary depending on the deck or patio. If the 4×4 posts are to rest on a wood deck or concrete patio, a metal base can be anchored into the surface with 16-penny or concrete nails. In other situations, precast pier blocks make good footings.

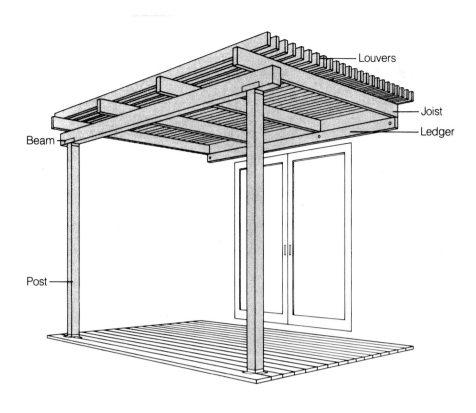

Beam

Louvers

Joist

Ledger

Post

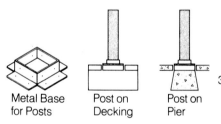

Metal Base for Posts   Post on Decking   Post on Pier

Trim posts to the proper height. (See below.) The top of the posts should be the same height as the ledger, minus the width of the beam. Measure the actual width of the timber you are using. The actual dimensions of a surfaced 4×6 will be close to 3½×5½ inches. Be sure to make allowance for the metal base and post cap.

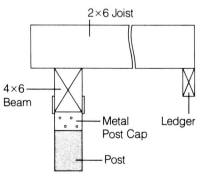

2×6 Joist

4×6 Beam

Metal Post Cap

Ledger

Post

Anchor the posts to their bases or footing with 8d nails. Plumb the posts with a carpenter's level and use temporary supporting boards to hold them in position while you complete the shelter's construction.

3 **Beam** Attach the metal post caps and secure the 4×6 beam with 8d nails.

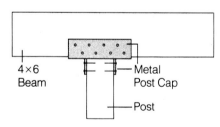

4×6 Beam

Metal Post Cap

Post

4 **Joists** Install joists at no more than four-foot intervals and toenail to the ledger and beam with 8d nails. If your measurements were accurate, joists should be level. If possible, nail joists to part of the eaves as this will restrict lateral movement of the shelter.

5 **Louvers** Toenail 1×4 louvers in place. The distance between the louvers will determine the degree of shade or sun. For moderate filtered sunlight, place louvers about 4 inches on center. If, after your shelter is complete, you find it needs more stability, add 2×4 corner braces from the beam to each post.

Shelter Materials

Description	Quantity	Size	Length
Construction Heart Redwood			
Posts	2	4×4	8 feet
Ledger	1	2×4	12 feet
Construction Common Redwood			
Beam	1	4×6	12 feet
Joists	4	2×6	8 feet
Louvers	24	1×4	12 feet

Other Materials

Quantity	Description
2	Metal bases for posts
2	Metal caps for posts
4	⅜×6 inch lag screws for ledger
1 lb.	8 penny nails for beam, joists & louvers
¼ lb.	16 penny nails for metal base (wood deck)
¼ lb.	Concrete nails for metal base (concrete patio)

Use non-corrosive, hot-dipped galvanized, stainless steel, or aluminum fasteners and hardware.

Butcherblock Bench

Redwood butcherblock benches are stylish additions to redwood decks or garden patios. These benches can be nail-laminated in different lengths using economical garden grades of redwood. Construction Heart or Deck Heart should be used for bench legs and where increased decay resistance is needed. Construction Common, Deck Common or Merchantable may be used for seats.

To keep the seats even and level, build benches on edge or upside down on a flat surface. For top performance, use non-corrosive nails and hardware: stainless steel, aluminum or top quality, hot-dipped galvanized. To prevent splitting, predrill nail holes near board ends.

This bench is made entirely of 2x4's. There are two basic elements: the legs and the seat.

Legs are built up with two 2x4's—one long piece and one short. Trim four long pieces so that they are 18 inches long. Trim four short pieces to 14½ inches. To make legs, assemble short and long pieces in pairs with six 8-penny nails.

Seatboards are made by nail-laminating ten 2x4's together, creating the butcherblock appearance. The length of the 2x4's used for the seat will vary according to the length of the bench. (See materials lists.) Trim two short pieces to accommodate the legs. Make sure the 2x4's are level and even on the top seating area. Use 12-penny nails and nail every 6 inches in a zig-zag pattern. The seat may be planed after construction to even the seating surface.

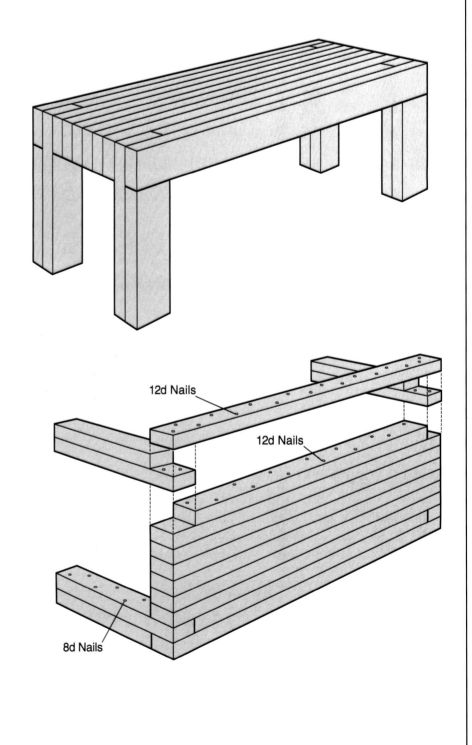

Materials Lists

Bench Length	Lumber 2x4
4 feet	2 pcs. 6' 5 pcs. 8'
6 feet	12 pcs. 6'
8 feet	10 pcs. 8' 2 pcs. 6'
10 feet	10 pcs. 10' 2 pcs. 6'
12 feet	10 pcs.12' 2 pcs. 6'
Nails	8-penny nails 12-penny nails

Redwood 4×4 Planter Construction Tips

This handsome planter will enliven a deck, garden or patio. Use Construction Heart for pieces in contact with soil.

For best results: Measure and trim each piece as you build. Predrill holes, especially at the ends of boards to prevent splitting. Use only top-quality, hot-dipped galvanized nails to prevent stains.

1 Nail two 2×2's to adjacent faces of each 4×4 corner post. Use 12d nails. Leave room for the 1×4 panels to fit flush with outer faces of the 4×4 posts.

2 Attach 1×4 boards to posts with two 6d nails at each board end. The 1×4 boards should be evenly spaced along the post and flush with the bottom and outer face. Use Construction Heart for interior walls.

3 Complete two walls, both inside and out, to form an "L" as shown in the illustration. Then construct the last two walls, completing the box. It may help to lay the project on its side when nailing the last walls.

4 For the base, turn the box upside down and place 2×4's on opposite sides, 1-inch in from the edge. With two 12d nails in each board end, attach the 2×4's to the 4×4 posts. Drill two 1-inch drainage holes in two of the 2×6's to be used for the bottom. Turn the box upright and lay all four 2×6's in place to form the bottom of the planter.

5 For the top trim, butt-join 1×4's flush with the planter's outer edge. Use two 6d nails at each board end, penetrating the 4×4 at one end and the 2×2 at the other. These nails can be countersunk and filled with non-oily wood filler.

6 Interior surfaces should be lined with a polyethylene liner. Make sure to provide proper drainage by cutting holes through the bottom of the planter and the liner.

Planter Materials

Construction Heart/Deck Heart*

4×4	4 pieces	15"
1×4	16 pieces	22 ½"
2×6	4 pieces	22 ½"
2×4	2 pieces	24 ½"

Construction Common/Deck Common*

1×4	16 pieces	22 ½"
1×4	4 pieces	26 ½"
2×2	8 pieces	15"

Nails

60	12-penny
160	6-penny

*Deck Heart and Deck Common are available in 2×4 and 2×6 only.

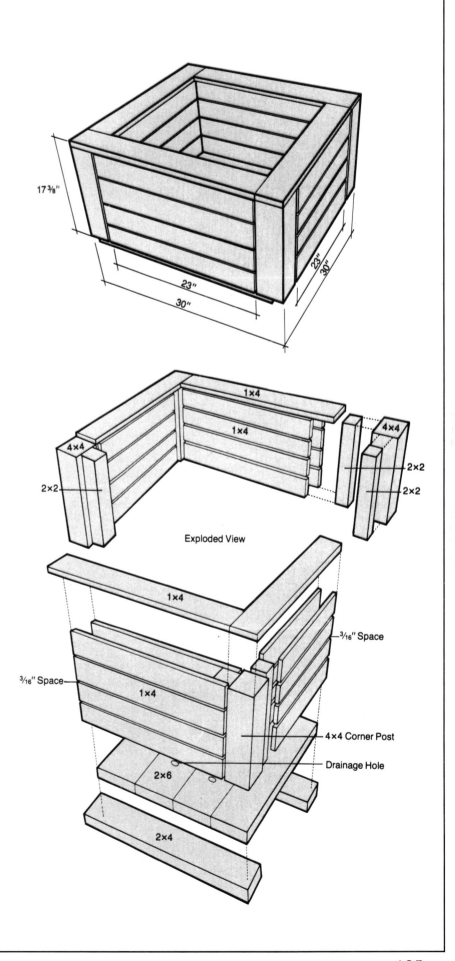

Exploded View

17 ⅜" 23" 30" 23" 30"

1×4 4×4 2×2 2×2 2×2

1×4 ³⁄₁₆" Space ³⁄₁₆" Space 4×4 Corner Post Drainage Hole 2×6 2×4

Cut-out Deck Modules

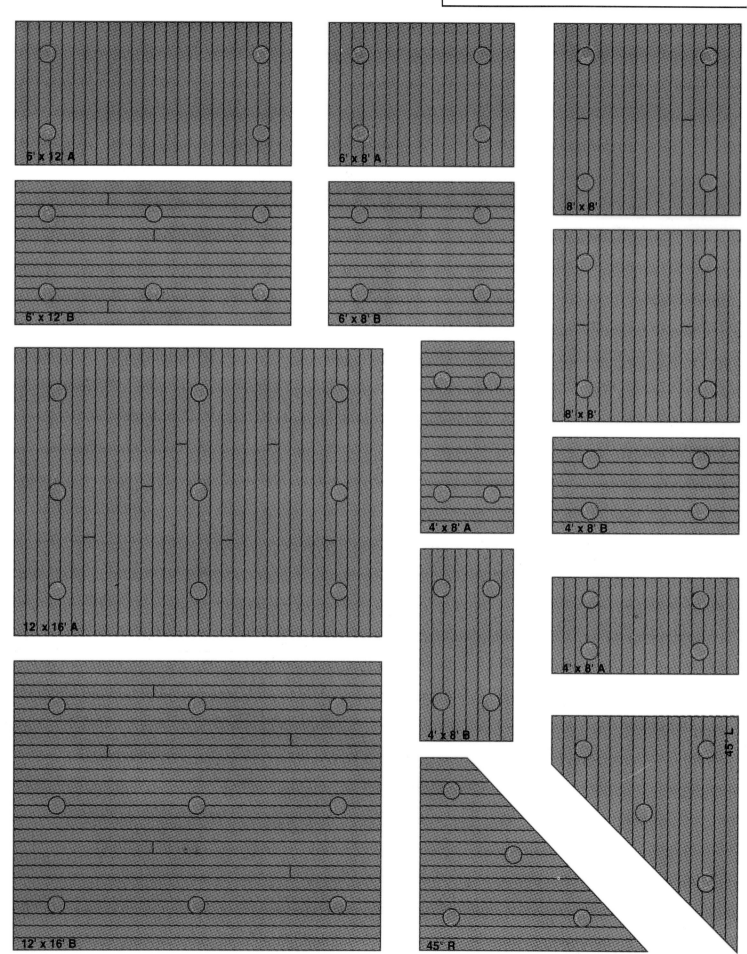

6' x 12' A

6' x 8' A

8' x 8'

6' x 12' B

6' x 8' B

8' x 8'

4' x 8' A

4' x 8' B

12' x 16' A

4' x 8' A

4' x 8' B

45° L

12' x 16' B

45° R

Scale: 1/4" = 1 foot

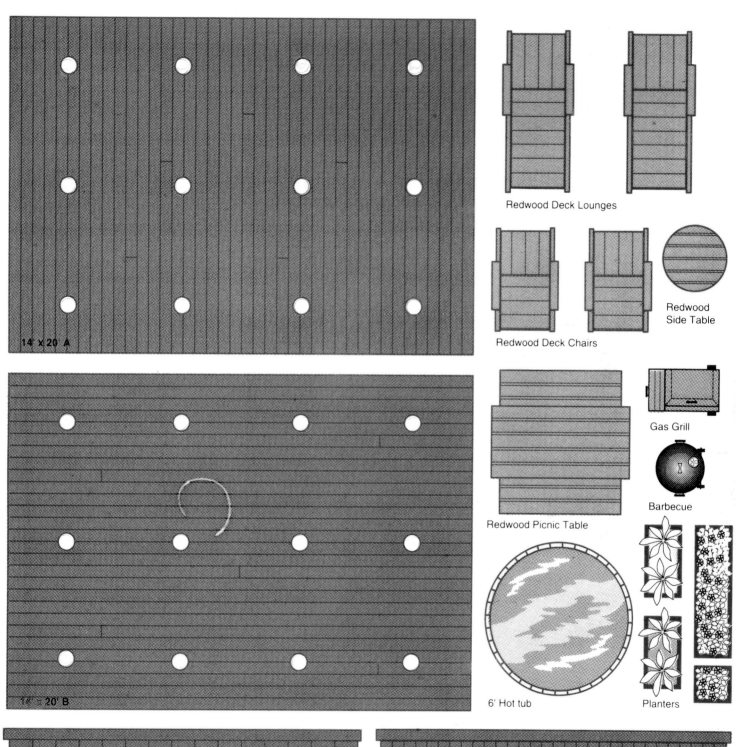

14' x 20' A

14' x 20' B

Redwood Deck Lounges

Redwood Deck Chairs

Redwood
Side Table

Gas Grill

Barbecue

Redwood Picnic Table

6' Hot tub

Planters

3' Stairs—trim length as needed.

These stair forms are provided to help you indicate stair locations.
Refer to Section D of the Deck Construction Guide, page 21 for
proper stair construction.

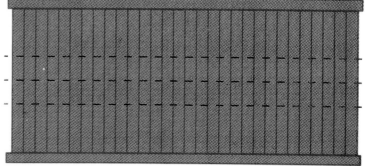

6' Stairs—cut along the black dotted lines to create other stair widths, such
as 4' and 5', by overlapping the pieces. Trim the length as needed.

Scale: ¼" = 1 foot

Deck Construction
Overview

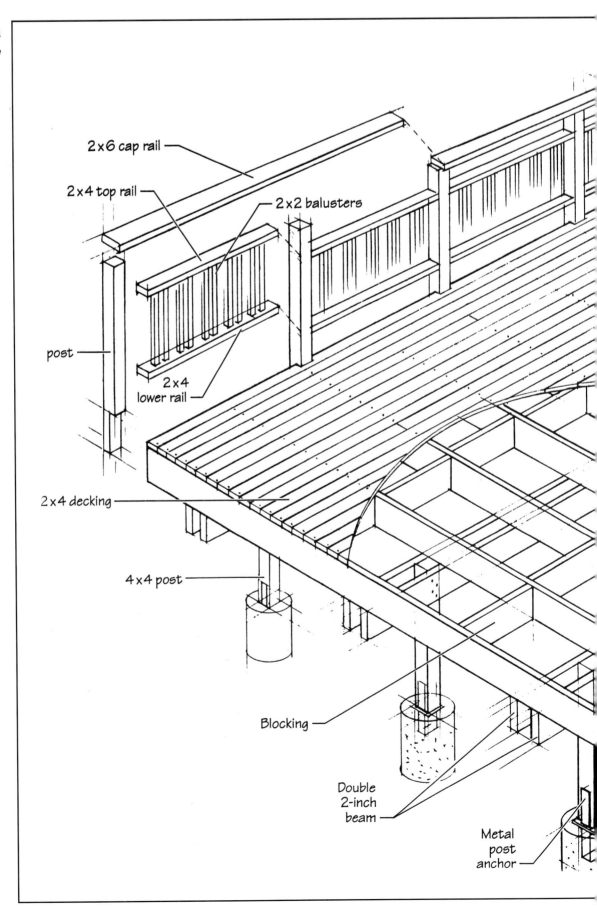

2 x 6 cap rail

2 x 4 top rail

2 x 2 balusters

post

2 x 4
lower rail

2 x 4 decking

4 x 4 post

Blocking

Double
2-inch
beam

Metal
post
anchor

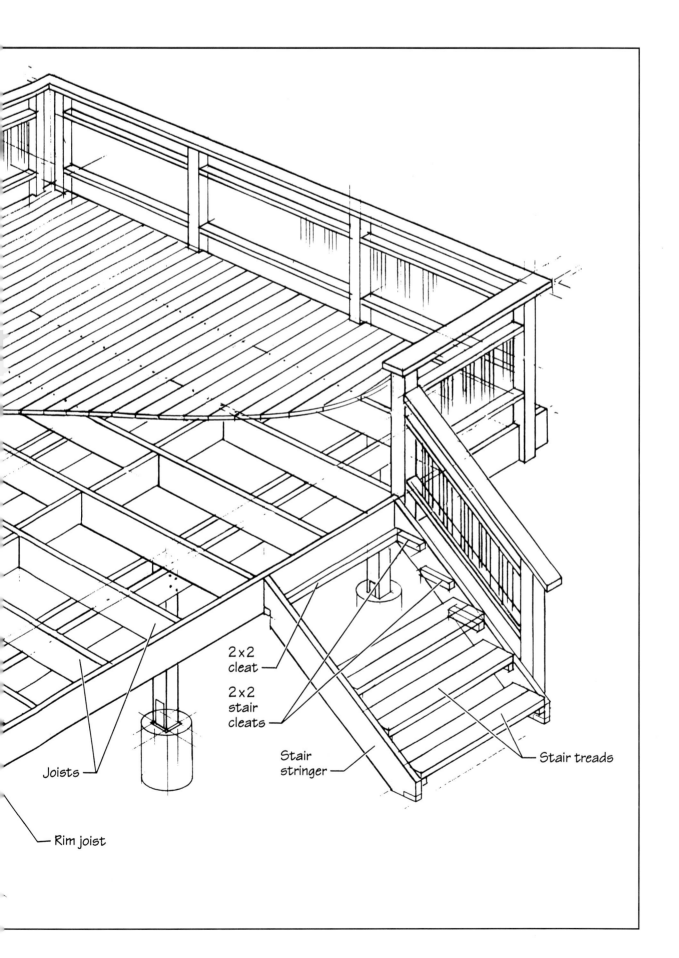

2 x 2 cleat

2 x 2 stair cleats

Stair stringer

Stair treads

Joists

Rim joist

Bracing details

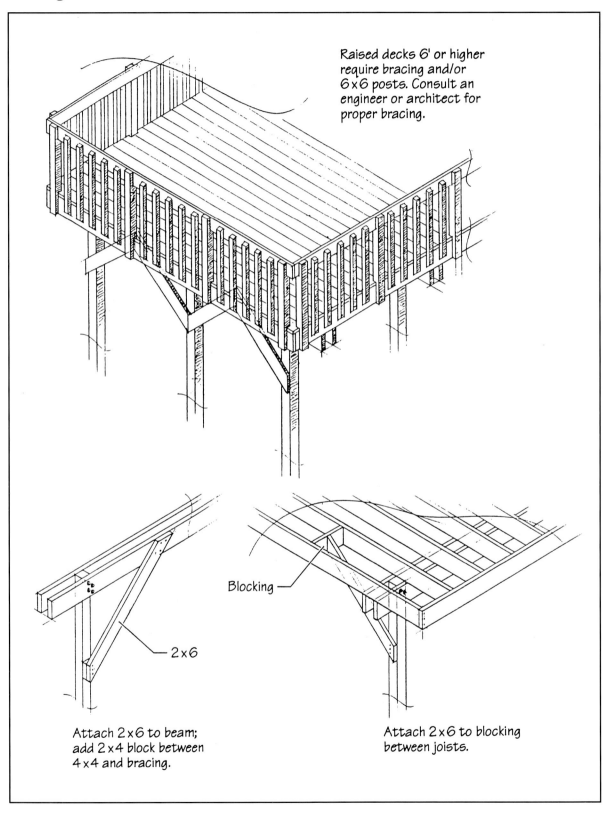

Raised decks 6' or higher require bracing and/or 6 x 6 posts. Consult an engineer or architect for proper bracing.

2 x 6

Blocking

Attach 2 x 6 to beam; add 2 x 4 block between 4 x 4 and bracing.

Attach 2 x 6 to blocking between joists.

Cut-out Module Blueprints

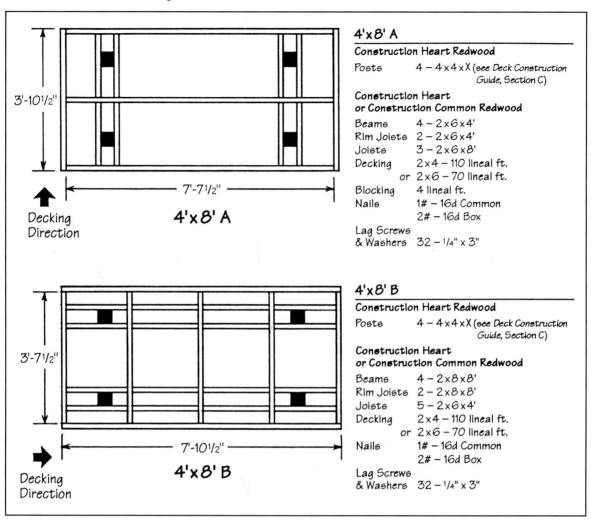

3'-10½"

7'-7½"

4'x8' A

Decking Direction

4'x8' A

Construction Heart Redwood

Posts	4 – 4 x 4 x X (see Deck Construction Guide, Section C)

Construction Heart or Construction Common Redwood

Beams	4 – 2 x 6 x 4'
Rim Joists	2 – 2 x 6 x 4'
Joists	3 – 2 x 6 x 8'
Decking	2 x 4 – 110 lineal ft.
	or 2 x 6 – 70 lineal ft.
Blocking	4 lineal ft.
Nails	1# – 16d Common
	2# – 16d Box
Lag Screws & Washers	32 – ¼" x 3"

3'-7½"

7'-10½"

4'x8' B

Decking Direction

4'x8' B

Construction Heart Redwood

Posts	4 – 4 x 4 x X (see Deck Construction Guide, Section C)

Construction Heart or Construction Common Redwood

Beams	4 – 2 x 8 x 8'
Rim Joists	2 – 2 x 8 x 8'
Joists	5 – 2 x 6 x 4'
Decking	2 x 4 – 110 lineal ft.
	or 2 x 6 – 70 lineal ft.
Nails	1# – 16d Common
	2# – 16d Box
Lag Screws & Washers	32 – ¼" x 3"

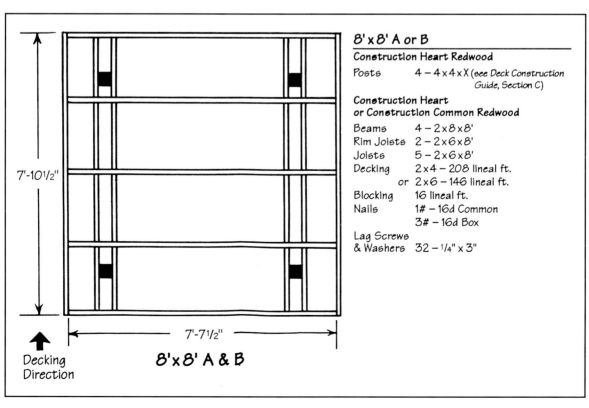

7'-10½"

7'-7½"

8'x8' A & B

Decking Direction

8'x8' A or B

Construction Heart Redwood

Posts	4 – 4 x 4 x X (see Deck Construction Guide, Section C)

Construction Heart or Construction Common Redwood

Beams	4 – 2 x 8 x 8'
Rim Joists	2 – 2 x 6 x 8'
Joists	5 – 2 x 6 x 8'
Decking	2 x 4 – 208 lineal ft.
	or 2 x 6 – 146 lineal ft.
Blocking	16 lineal ft.
Nails	1# – 16d Common
	3# – 16d Box
Lag Screws & Washers	32 – ¼" x 3"

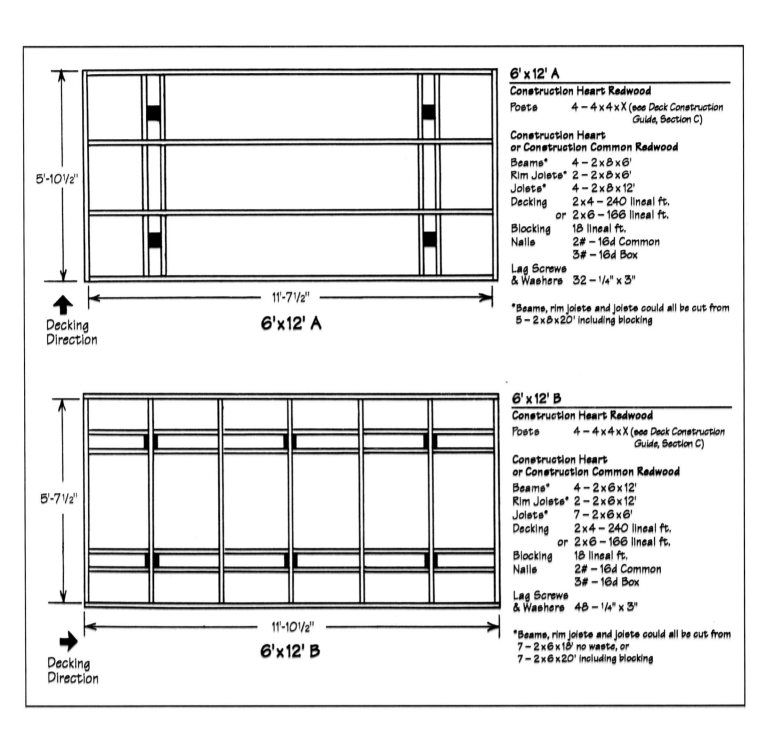

Decking Direction (for 6'x12' A)

5'-10½"

11'-7½"

6'x12' A

6' x 12' A

Construction Heart Redwood

Posts	4 – 4 x 4 x X (see Deck Construction Guide, Section C)

Construction Heart or Construction Common Redwood

Beams*	4 – 2 x 8 x 6'
Rim Joists*	2 – 2 x 8 x 6'
Joists*	4 – 2 x 8 x 12'
Decking	2 x 4 – 240 lineal ft.
	or 2 x 6 – 166 lineal ft.
Blocking	18 lineal ft.
Nails	2# – 16d Common
	3# – 16d Box
Lag Screws & Washers	32 – ¼" x 3"

*Beams, rim joists and joists could all be cut from 5 – 2 x 8 x 20' including blocking

Decking Direction (for 6'x12' B)

5'-7½"

11'-10½"

6'x12' B

6' x 12' B

Construction Heart Redwood

Posts	4 – 4 x 4 x X (see Deck Construction Guide, Section C)

Construction Heart or Construction Common Redwood

Beams*	4 – 2 x 6 x 12'
Rim Joists*	2 – 2 x 6 x 12'
Joists*	7 – 2 x 6 x 6'
Decking	2 x 4 – 240 lineal ft.
	or 2 x 6 – 166 lineal ft.
Blocking	18 lineal ft.
Nails	2# – 16d Common
	3# – 16d Box
Lag Screws & Washers	48 – ¼" x 3"

*Beams, rim joists and joists could all be cut from
7 – 2 x 6 x 18' no waste, or
7 – 2 x 6 x 20' including blocking

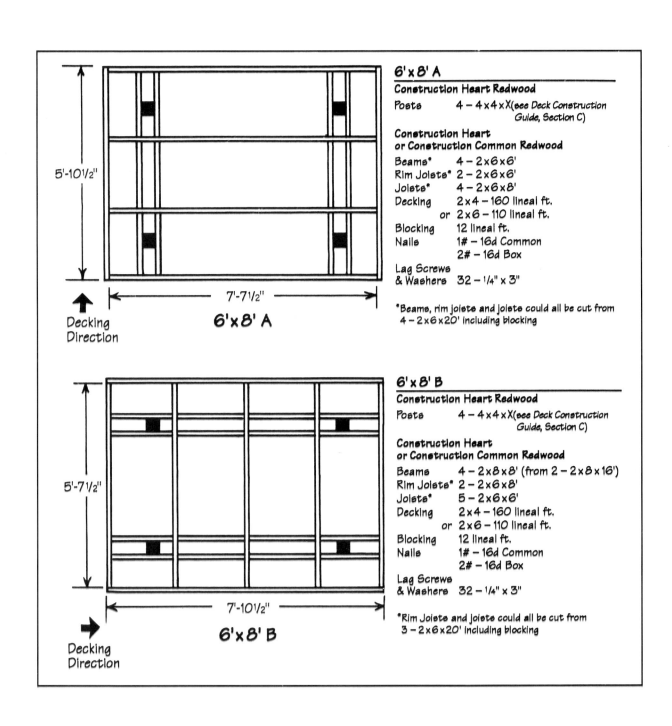

5'-10½"

7'-7½"

6'x8' A

Decking
Direction

6' x 8' A

Construction Heart Redwood

Posts	4 – 4 x 4 x X (see Deck Construction Guide, Section C)

**Construction Heart
or Construction Common Redwood**

Beams*	4 – 2 x 6 x 6'
Rim Joists*	2 – 2 x 6 x 6'
Joists*	4 – 2 x 6 x 8'
Decking	2 x 4 – 160 lineal ft.
	or 2 x 6 – 110 lineal ft.
Blocking	12 lineal ft.
Nails	1# – 16d Common
	2# – 16d Box
Lag Screws & Washers	32 – ¼" x 3"

*Beams, rim joists and joists could all be cut from
 4 – 2 x 6 x 20' including blocking

5'-7½"

7'-10½"

6'x8' B

Decking
Direction

6' x 8' B

Construction Heart Redwood

Posts	4 – 4 x 4 x X (see Deck Construction Guide, Section C)

**Construction Heart
or Construction Common Redwood**

Beams	4 – 2 x 8 x 8' (from 2 – 2 x 8 x 16')
Rim Joists*	2 – 2 x 6 x 8'
Joists*	5 – 2 x 6 x 6'
Decking	2 x 4 – 160 lineal ft.
	or 2 x 6 – 110 lineal ft.
Blocking	12 lineal ft.
Nails	1# – 16d Common
	2# – 16d Box
Lag Screws & Washers	32 – ¼" x 3"

*Rim Joists and joists could all be cut from
 3 – 2 x 6 x 20' including blocking

143

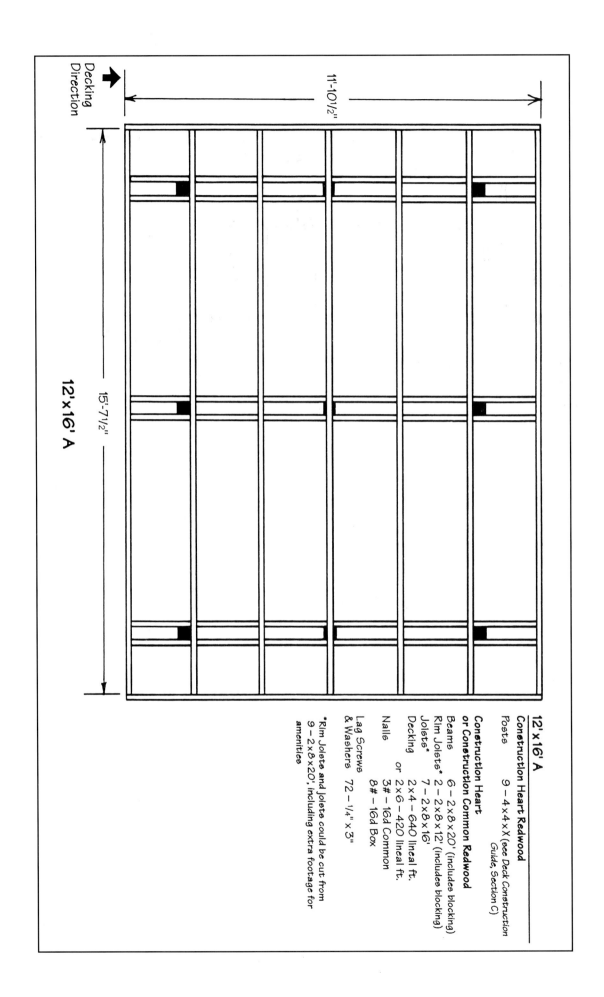

Decking Direction

11'-10½"

12'x16' A

15'-7½"

12'x16' A

Construction Heart Redwood

Posts   9 — 4 x 4 x X (see Deck Construction Guide, Section C)

Construction Heart or Construction Common Redwood

Beams   6 — 2 x 8 x 20' (includes blocking)
Rim Joists* 2 — 2 x 8 x 12' (includes blocking)
Joists*   7 — 2 x 8 x 16'
Decking   2 x 4 — 640 lineal ft.
    or 2 x 6 — 420 lineal ft.
Nails   3# — 16d Common
    8# — 16d Box
Lag Screws
& Washers 72 — 1/4" x 3"

*Rim Joists and Joists could be cut from 9 — 2 x 8 x 20', including extra footage for amenities

144

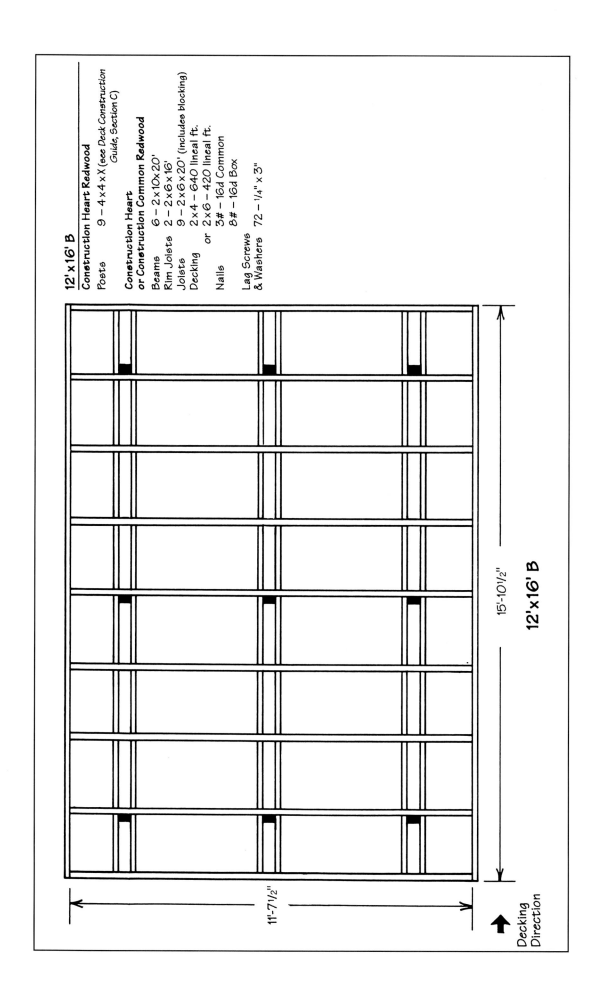

12'x16' B

Construction Heart Redwood

Posts   9 – 4 x 4 x X (see Deck Construction
                                              Guide, Section C)

**Construction Heart
or Construction Common Redwood**

Beams   6 – 2 x 10 x 20'
Rim Joists   2 – 2 x 6 x 16'
Joists   9 – 2 x 6 x 20' (includes blocking)
Decking   2 x 4 – 640 lineal ft.
        or   2 x 6 – 420 lineal ft.

Nails   3# – 16d Common
              8# – 16d Box

Lag Screws
& Washers   72 – 1/4" x 3"

15'-10½"

11'-7½"

12'x16' B

Decking
Direction

145

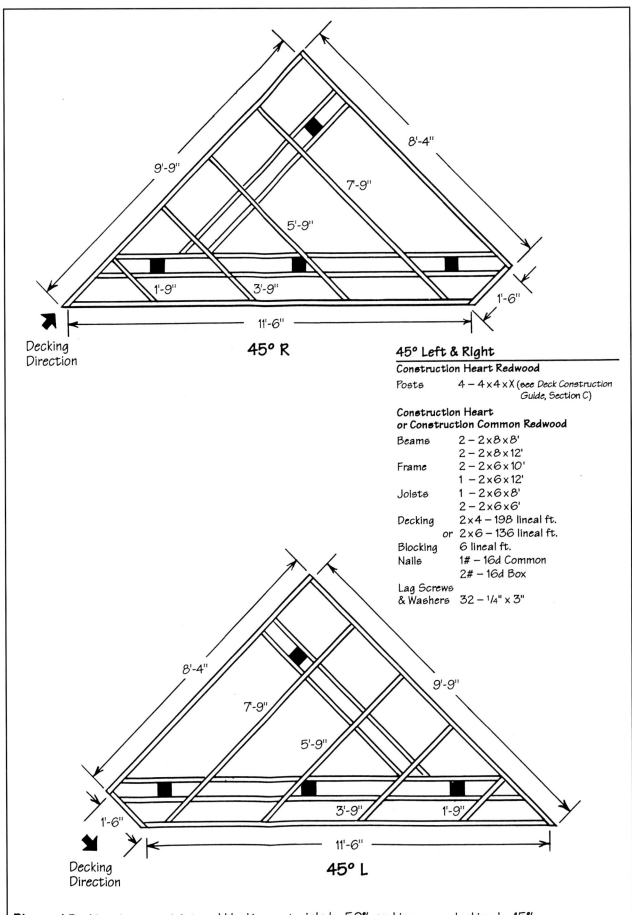

45° R

Decking Direction

45° Left & Right

Construction Heart Redwood

Posts	4 – 4 x 4 x X (see Deck Construction Guide, Section C)

Construction Heart or Construction Common Redwood

Beams	2 – 2 x 8 x 8'
	2 – 2 x 8 x 12'
Frame	2 – 2 x 6 x 10'
	1 – 2 x 6 x 12'
Joists	1 – 2 x 6 x 8'
	2 – 2 x 6 x 6'
Decking	2 x 4 – 198 lineal ft.
or	2 x 6 – 136 lineal ft.
Blocking	6 lineal ft.
Nails	1# – 16d Common
	2# – 16d Box
Lag Screws & Washers	32 – ¼" x 3"

45° L

Decking Direction

Diagonal Decking: Increase joist and blocking materials by 50% and increase decking by 15%. Install joists 16" o.c. Diagonal decking can be installed using either A or B framing plans.

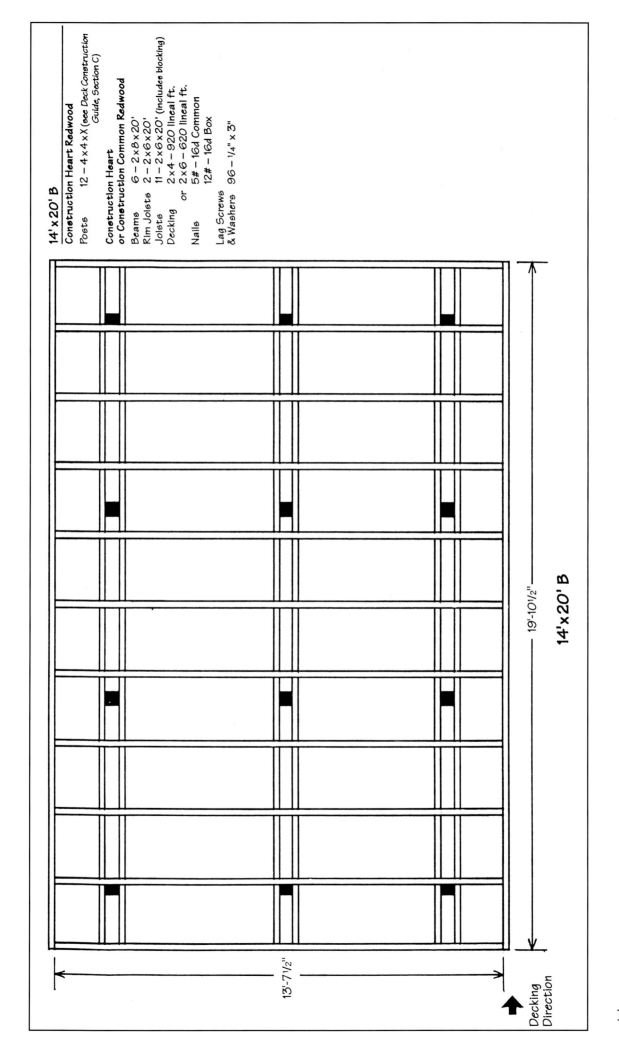

14' x 20' B

Construction Heart Redwood

Posts   12 – 4 x 4 x X (see Deck Construction
                              Guide, Section C)

Construction Heart
or Construction Common Redwood

Beams   6 – 2 x 8 x 20'
Rim Joists 2 – 2 x 6 x 20'
Joists   11 – 2 x 6 x 20' (includes blocking)
Decking   2 x 4 – 920 lineal ft.
      or   2 x 6 – 620 lineal ft.
Nails   5# – 16d Common
           12# – 16d Box

Lag Screws
& Washers 96 – ¼" x 3"

19'-10½"

13'-7½"

14'x 20' B

Decking
Direction

147

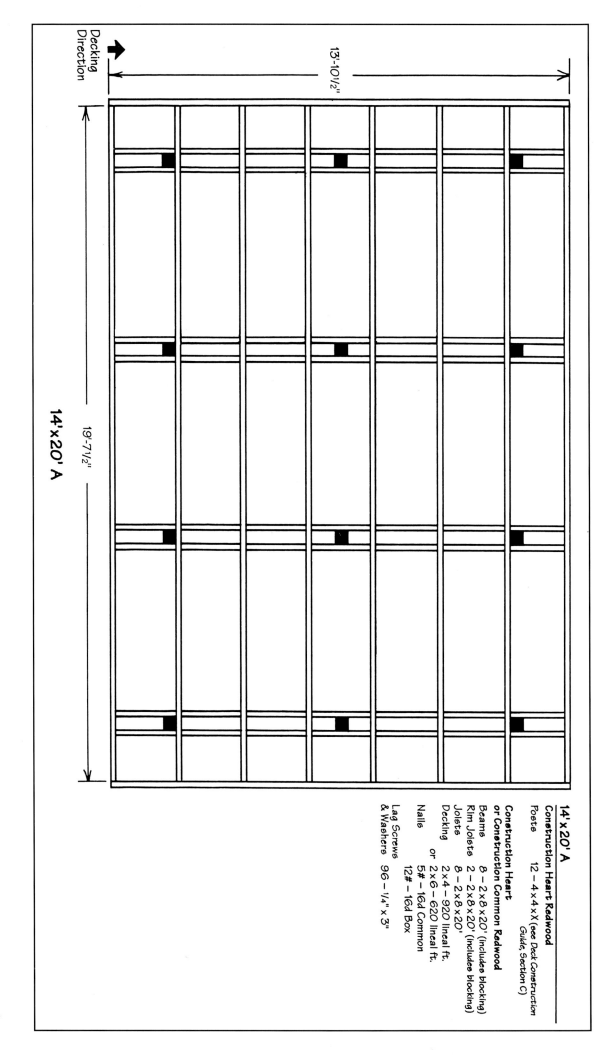

Decking Direction

13'-10½"

19'-7½"

14' x 20' A

14' x 20' A

Construction Heart Redwood

Posts   12 – 4 x 4 x X (see Deck Construction Guide, Section C)

Construction Heart or Construction Common Redwood

Beams   8 – 2 x 8 x 20' (includes blocking)
Rim Joists   2 – 2 x 8 x 20' (includes blocking)
Joists   8 – 2 x 8 x 20'
Decking   2 x 4 – 920 lineal ft.
     or   2 x 6 – 620 lineal ft.
Nails   5# – 16d Common
      12# – 16d Box
Lag Screws & Washers   96 – ¼" x 3"

Solid Stringer – *Section View*

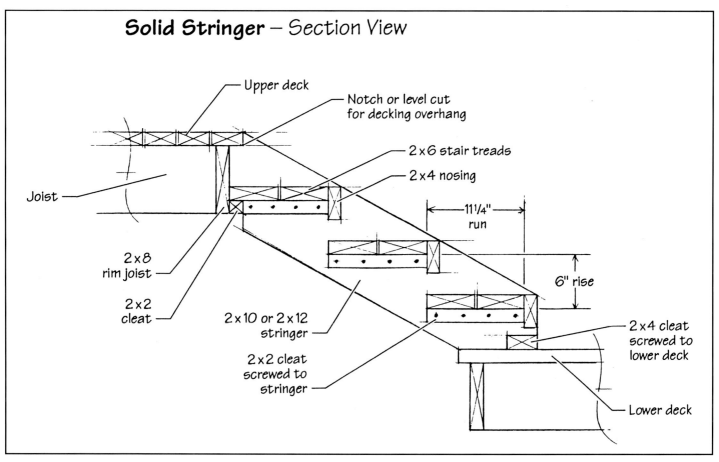

Upper deck

Notch or level cut
for decking overhang

2 x 6 stair treads

2 x 4 nosing

Joist

11¼"
run

6" rise

2 x 8
rim joist

2 x 2
cleat

2 x 10 or 2 x 12
stringer

2 x 4 cleat
screwed to
lower deck

2 x 2 cleat
screwed to
stringer

Lower deck

Solid Stringer – *Perspective View*

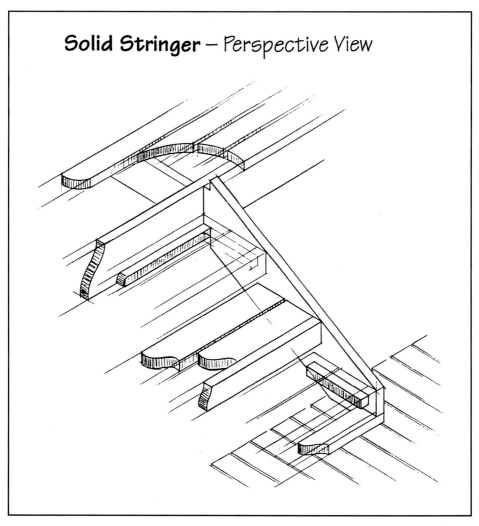

Cutout Stringer – Section View

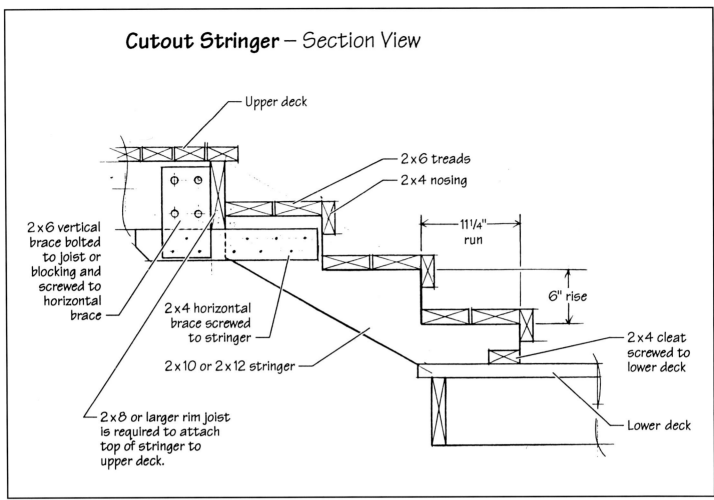

Upper deck

2 x 6 treads

2 x 4 nosing

11¼" run

6" rise

2 x 6 vertical brace bolted to joist or blocking and screwed to horizontal brace

2 x 4 horizontal brace screwed to stringer

2 x 10 or 2 x 12 stringer

2 x 8 or larger rim joist is required to attach top of stringer to upper deck.

2 x 4 cleat screwed to lower deck

Lower deck

Cutout Stringer – Perspective View

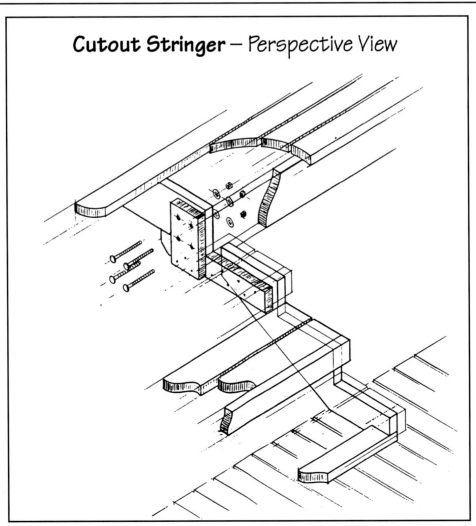

Stair Railing Attachment – Section View

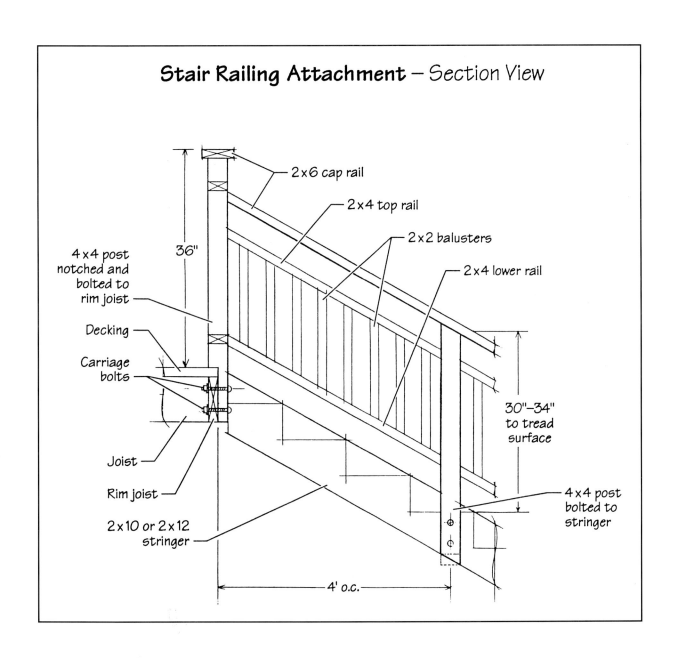

- 2 x 6 cap rail
- 2 x 4 top rail
- 2 x 2 balusters
- 2 x 4 lower rail

4 x 4 post notched and bolted to rim joist

36"

Decking

Carriage bolts

Joist

Rim joist

2 x 10 or 2 x 12 stringer

30"–34" to tread surface

4 x 4 post bolted to stringer

4' o.c.

Stair Railing Attachment – Perspective View

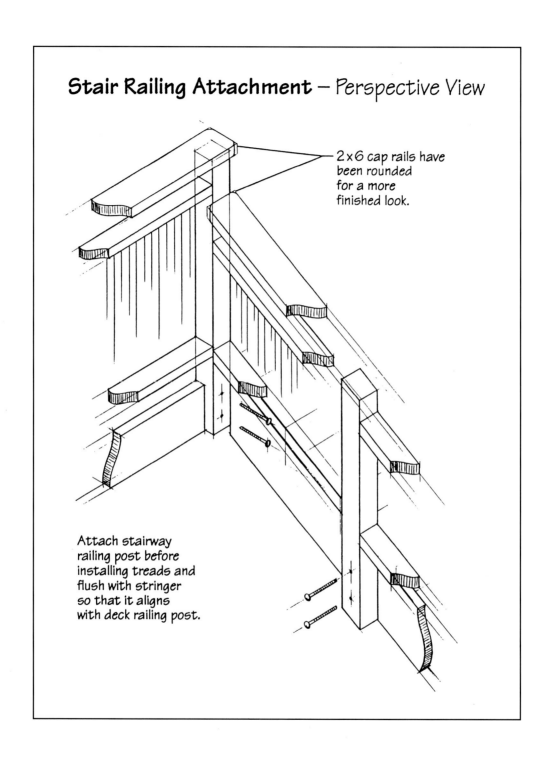

2 x 6 cap rails have been rounded for a more finished look.

Attach stairway railing post before installing treads and flush with stringer so that it aligns with deck railing post.

Solid Side Railing Options:

Diagonal (or Vertical)

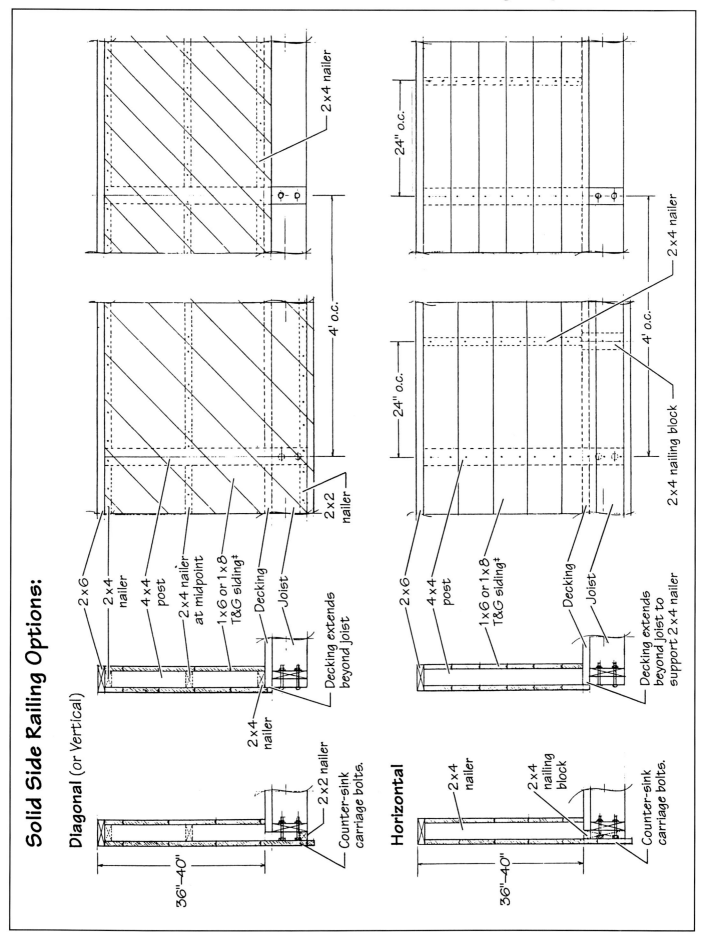

2×4 nailer

24" o.c.

4' o.c.

2×4 nailer

24" o.c.

4' o.c.

2×4 nailing block

2×2 nailer

2×6
2×4 nailer
4×4 post
2×4 nailer at midpoint
1×6 or 1×8 T&G siding‡
Decking
Joist
Decking extends beyond joist
2×4 nailer

2×6
4×4 post
1×6 or 1×8 T&G siding‡
Decking
Joist
Decking extends beyond joist to support 2×4 nailer

36"–40"

2×2 nailer
Counter-sink carriage bolts.

Horizontal

2×4 nailer
2×4 nailing block
Counter-sink carriage bolts.

36"–40"

Note: Materials are estimated for a single four-foot section. Use these lists as work sheets to obtain totals which can then be transferred to the Materials Work Sheet on page 7 of the *Deck Construction Guide*.

Additional posts and hardware that are required to complete the last four-foot section of your railing are itemized in the column marked: +*.

‡ For additional siding options refer to CRA's *Certified Kiln Dried Siding Patterns and Applications*.

Diagonal or Vertical Solid Side Railing

ITEM	Dimension	Qty.	x Sections	+ *	= TOTAL
Post	4 x 4 x 4'	1	x _____	+ 1	= _____
Cap Rail	2 x 6 x 4'6"	1	x _____		= _____
Nailers	2 x 4 x 4'	2	x _____		= _____
Tongue & Groove or Shiplap Siding	1 x 6'	42'	x _____		= _____
	1 x 8'	29'	x _____		= _____
(lineal feet, single side quantity)					
Carriage Bolts, Washers & Nuts	1/2" x 6"	2	x _____	+ 2	= _____
Other Hardware	1# common nails	1	x _____		= _____

Horizontal Solid Side Railing

ITEM	Dimension	Qty.	x Sections	+ *	= TOTAL
Post	4 x 4 x 4'	1	x _____	+ 1	= _____
Cap Rail	2 x 6 x 4'6"	1	x _____		= _____
Intermediate Post	2 x 4 x 3'	1	x _____		= _____
Tongue & Groove or Shiplap Siding	1 x 6'	36'	x _____		= _____
	1 x 8'	25'	x _____		= _____
(lineal feet, single side quantity)					
Carriage Bolts, Washers & Nuts	1/2" x 6"	2	x _____	+ 2	= _____
Other Hardware	1# common nails	1	x _____		= _____

2 x 2 Baluster Railing

ITEM	Dimension	Qty.	x Sections	+ *	= TOTAL
Post	4 x 4 x 4'	1	x _____	+ 1	= _____
Cap Rail	2 x 6 x 4'6"	1	x _____		= _____
Top & Lower Rails	2 x 4 x 4'	2	x _____		= _____
Even-spaced Balusters	2 x 2	20'	x _____		= _____
or					
Paired or Parallel Balusters (lineal feet)	2 x 2	18'	x _____		= _____
Carriage Bolts, Washers & Nuts	1/2" x 6"	2	x _____	+ 2	= _____
Other Hardware	1/2# wood screws or common nails	1	x _____		= _____

Cambered 2 x 2 Upright Baluster Railing

ITEM	Dimension	Qty.	x Sections	+ *	= TOTAL
Post	4 x 4 x 4'	1	x _____	+ 1	= _____
Top Rail	2 x 6 x 4'6"	1	x _____		= _____
Balusters	2 x 2 x 3'8"	8	x _____		= _____
Carriage Bolts, Washers & Nuts	1/2" x 6"	2	x _____	+ 2	= _____
Other Hardware	1/2# wood screws	1	x _____		= _____

Horizontal 2 x 2 Railing

ITEM	Dimension	Qty.	x Sections	+ *	= TOTAL
Post	4 x 4 x 4'	1	x _____	+ 1	= _____
Cap Rail	2 x 6 x 4'6"	1	x _____		= _____
Top & Lower Rails	2 x 4 x 4'	2	x _____		= _____
Intermediate Rails	2 x 2 x 4'	4	x _____		= _____
Balusters	2 x 2 x 3'	4	x _____		= _____
Carriage Bolts, Washers & Nuts	1/2" x 6"	2	x _____	+ 2	= _____
Other Hardware	1/2# wood screws or common nails	1	x _____		= _____

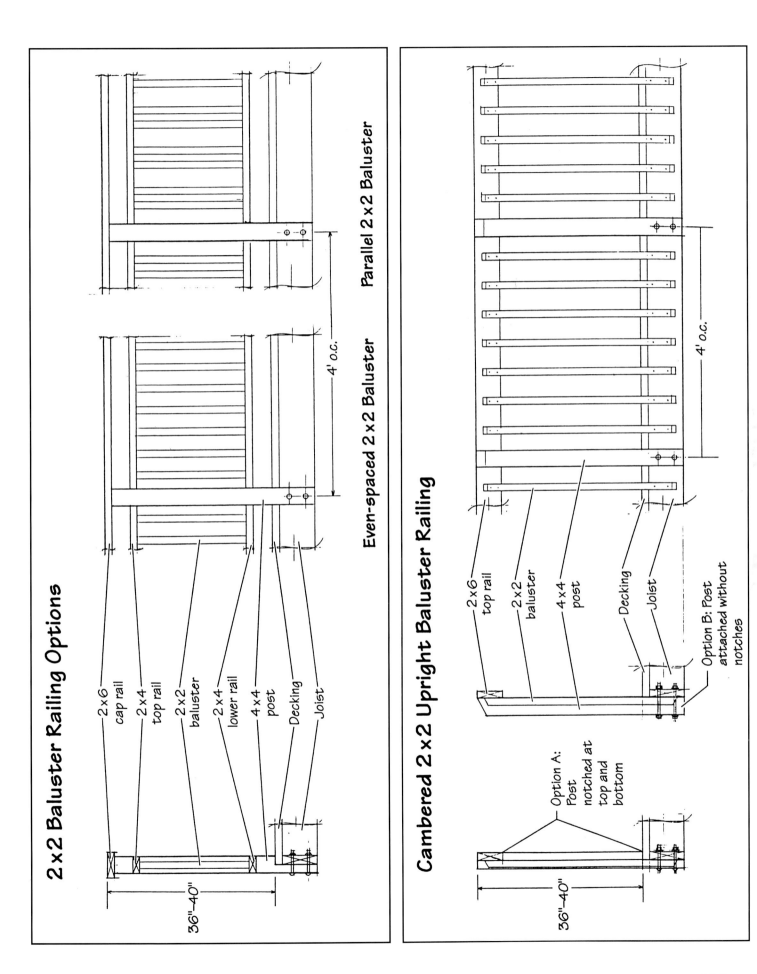

2x2 Baluster Railing Options

Parallel 2x2 Baluster

Even-spaced 2x2 Baluster

4' o.c.

2x6 cap rail
2x4 top rail
2x2 baluster
2x4 lower rail
4x4 post
Decking
Joist

36"–40"

Cambered 2x2 Upright Baluster Railing

4' o.c.

2x6 top rail
2x2 baluster
4x4 post
Decking
Joist

Option B: Post attached without notches

Option A: Post notched at top and bottom

36"–40"

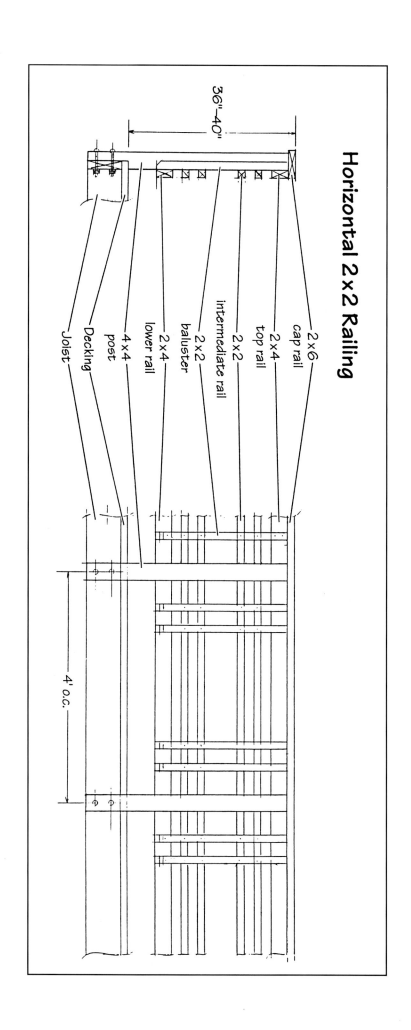

Horizontal 2x2 Railing

36"-40"

2x6
cap rail

2x4
top rail

2x2
intermediate rail

2x2
baluster

2x4
lower rail

4x4
post

Decking

Joist

4' o.c.

Bench and Bench Railing Blueprints

Note: Materials are estimated for a single four-foot section. Use these lists as work sheets to obtain totals which can then be transferred to the Materials Work Sheet on page 7 of the *Deck Construction Guide*.

Additional posts, supports and other materials that are required to complete the last four-foot section of your bench are itemized in the column marked: +*.

Recommended Redwood Lumber Grades:
Construction Common, Construction Heart
Deck Common, Deck Heart
Clear All Heart, Clear or B Grade
See page 6 of the *Deck Construction Guide* for more information.

Through-deck Bench, no railing

ITEM	Dimension	Qty.	x Sections	+ *	= TOTAL
Post	4 x 4 x 2'	1	x _____	+ 1 =	_____
Seat Support	2 x 4 x 17"	2	x _____	+ 2 =	_____
Seat Rails	2 x 2 x 4'6"	8	x _____	=	_____
Rail Spacers	1 x 1 x 6½"	7	x _____	+ 7 =	_____
Carriage Bolts, Washers & Nuts	½" x 6"	2	x _____	+ 2 =	_____
Lag Screws & Washers	⅜" x 4"	4	x _____	+ 4 =	_____
Other Hardware	½# wood screws or nails	1	x _____	=	_____

Upright Bench & Railing

ITEM	Dimension	Qty.	x Sections	+ *	= TOTAL
Post	4 x 4 x 4'	1	x _____	+ 1 =	_____
Seat Support Post	4 x 4 x 2'	1	x _____	+ 1 =	_____
Seat Support	2 x 4 x 2'	2	x _____	+ 2 =	_____
Seat Rails	2 x 4 x 4'6"	4	x _____	=	_____
Seat Back Rails	2 x 4 x 4'6"	4	x _____	=	_____
Top Rail	2 x 6 x 4'6"	1	x _____	=	_____
Carriage Bolts, Washers & Nuts	½" x 6"	2	x _____	+ 2 =	_____
Lag Screws & Washers	⅜" x 4"	10	x _____	+ 10 =	_____
Other Hardware	½# wood screws or nails	1	x _____	=	_____

Angled-back Bench, Attached to Railing

ITEM	Dimension	Qty.	x Sections	+ *	= TOTAL
Post	4 x 4 x 2'	1	x _____	+ 1 =	_____
Seat Support Post	4 x 4 x 2'	1	x _____	+ 1 =	_____
Seat Support	4 x 4 x 2'	1	x _____	+ 1 =	_____
Seat Back Support	2 x 6 x 3'	2	x _____	+ 2 =	_____
Seat Rails	2 x 4 x 4'6"	2	x _____	=	_____
	2 x 2 x 4'6"	3	x _____	=	_____
Seat Back Rails	2 x 4 x 4'6"	2	x _____	=	_____
	2 x 2 x 4'6"	3	x _____	=	_____
Top Rail	2 x 6 x 4'6"	1	x _____	=	_____
Carriage Bolts, Washers & Nuts	½" x 6"	2	x _____	+ 2 =	_____
Lag Screws & Washers	⅜" x 4"	6	x _____	+ 6 =	_____
Other Hardware	½# wood screws or nails	1	x _____	=	_____

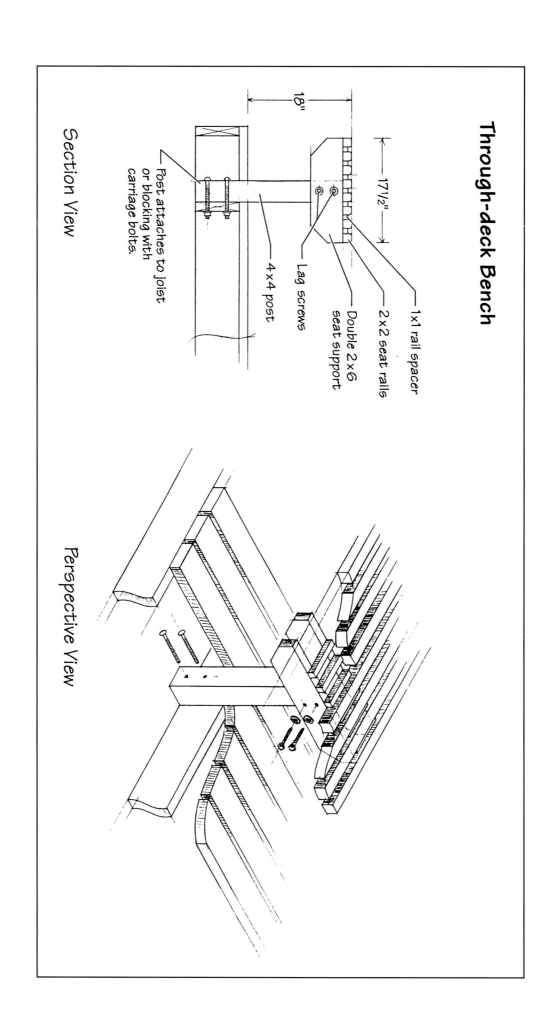

Through-deck Bench

18"

17 1/2"

1 x 1 rail spacer

2 x 2 seat rails

Double 2 x 6
seat support

Lag screws

4 x 4 post

Post attaches to joist
or blocking with
carriage bolts.

Section View

Perspective View

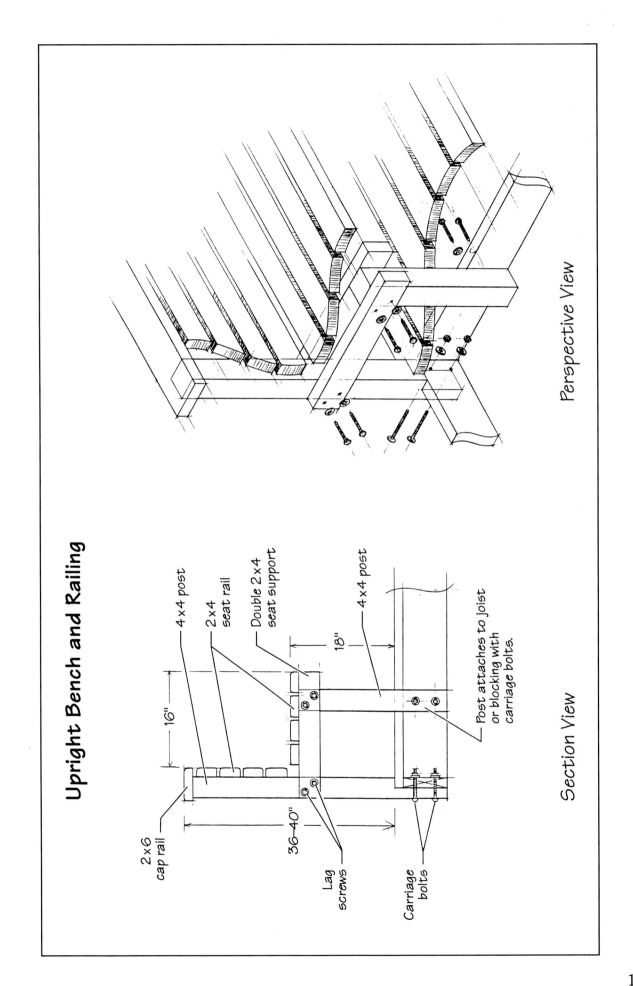

Upright Bench and Railing

2×6 cap rail

4×4 post

2×4 seat rail

Double 2×4 seat support

16"

18"

4×4 post

36-40"

Lag screws

Carriage bolts

Post attaches to joist or blocking with carriage bolts.

Section View

Perspective View

Angled-back Bench

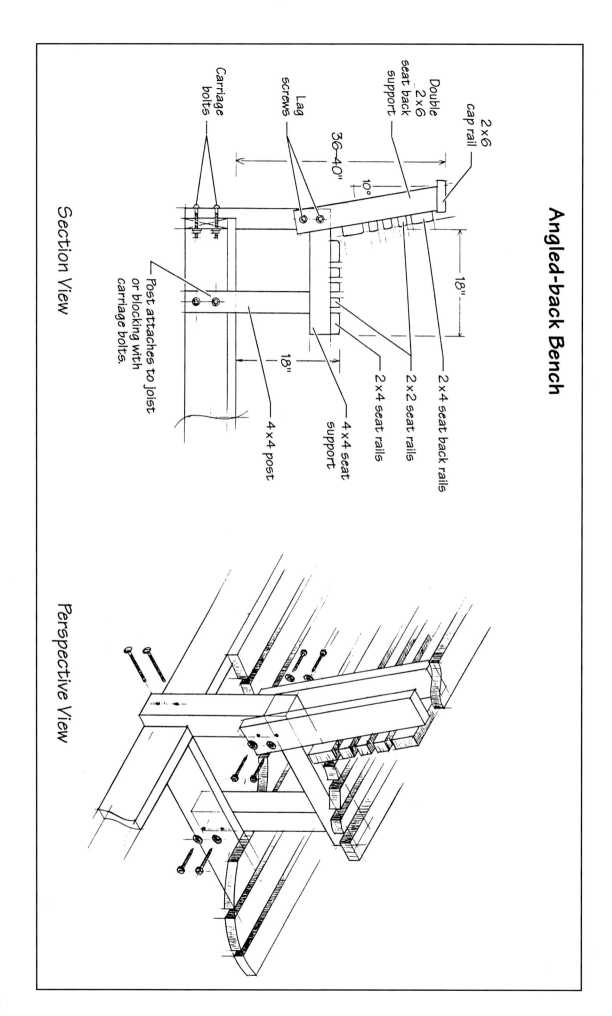

2×6 cap rail

Double 2×6 seat back support

Lag screws

Carriage bolts

36-40"

10°

18"

18"

Post attaches to joist or blocking with carriage bolts.

2×4 seat back rails

2×2 seat rails

2×4 seat rails

4×4 seat support

4×4 post

Section View

Perspective View